Riding Towards the Light

Riding Towards the Light

*An Apprenticeship
in the Art of Dressage Riding*

PAUL BELASIK

J. A. ALLEN
London

First published in Great Britain by
J. A. Allen & Co. Ltd
1 Lower Grosvenor Place
London
SW1W 0EL
1990

British Library Cataloguing in Publication Data
Belasik, Paul
 Riding towards the light: an apprenticeship in the art of
 dressage riding.
 1. Livestock: Horses. Riding. Dressage
 I. Title
 798.23

 ISBN 0-85131-509-7

Phototypeset by Input Typesetting Ltd, London
Printed and bound by
Billings and Sons Ltd, Worcester

Contents

I would like to dedicate this book to Henri Van Schaik. I know that I speak for many people of my generation when I thank him for cultivating in us an appreciation of the art in riding. Even more important for me has been his challenging insistence that we 'joust' with him.

Foreword

by
Erik F. Herbermann

ANY RIDER WHO has tangled at all seriously with the task of discovering the deep mysteries of horsemanship, will readily be able to identify with Paul Belasik's account of his journey through the bowels of an equestrian Hades in his search for truth about the horse. In this compelling and informative book, written in a delightfully frank style, Belasik shares his personal experiences of the unconventional and divergent paths he travelled. From masters of martial arts to masters of horsemanship, he sought out the common thread of fundamental values, and attempted to apply these in his own riding.

Important technicalities, such as the half-halt, balance, and the correlation of the seat and position and its effects on the horse, are all addressed with insight. I feel, however, that the most significant contribution is the thought-provoking philosophical dimension which will give readers a fresh perspective on riding, together with renewed hope and encouragement, and a sense of fellow-ship in the awareness that others too have made the arduous trek, and have known its doubts, and its joys and frustrations.

In today's highly technical equestrian world a book such as this one is very welcome indeed. It fills a con-siderable void, as food for the mind and spirit of man, as he discovers himself via the horse.

Preface

MANY YEARS AGO a monk was coming out of a monastery that was under the leadership of the great Zen man, Rinzai. Halfway across a bridge over a river, he met some monks from another Buddhist school. One of the monks stopped him and, referring to the river below, asked, 'How deep is the river of Zen?' The Zen monk, who was just returning from a session with Rinzai, a teacher legendary for his direct actions, without the slightest hesitation replied, 'Find out for yourself,' and began to throw the monk off the bridge. Fortunately he was saved by his two friends, who persuaded the first monk to stop.

To quote D. T. Suzuki: 'Zen is not necessarily against words, but it is well aware of the fact that they are always liable to detach themselves from realities and turn into conceptions. And this conceptualisation is what Zen is against. The Zen monk cited above may seem an extreme case but the spirit is there. Zen insists on handling the thing itself and not an empty abstraction.'[1]

With the tone of Zen's advice ringing in the air, I am going to try to recount my own apprenticeship in riding horses and particularly in the art of dressage. These words, apart from actual riding, are really meaningless. Perhaps they will mislead, or confuse, maybe encourage, but only the rider can enlighten him- or herself.

Dressage is from the French word for training. Above all, dressage is the systematic training of the horse to become stronger, more supple, and graceful. To a certain extent it is not an esoteric ballet-like endeavour, although it can look this way. Essentially it was born out of a highly practical matter. Namely, once a horse is mounted by a rider, its normal balance and centre of gravity are disturbed, to the point where the horse can prematurely damage itself with wear. Through systematic exercise and procedures dressage aims to remedy this imbalance, to train the horse to rebalance itself with the weight of the rider.

There is another element of dressage that cannot be glossed over. It is the pervasive connection it has with war, warriors and violence, primarily because of the horse's historic role in battle. At the Spanish Riding School in Vienna some of the most difficult movements

[1] SUZUKI, DAISETZ T., *Zen and Japanese Culture*, Bollingen Series, Princeton University Press, 1959.

practised today are living baroque representations of the evasive moves in battle – specialised kicks while in the air, controlled rears and so on. At Saumur in France, the famed Cadre Noir still perform ritualised battle movements in unison. In the bull rings of Portugal, exquisite horses perform spins, lifts, and passes with technical perfection, not technically perfect under the luxury of exhibition, but because improper execution may mean death.

Yet there is something in riding which is very close to the paradox which led the sword masters and Samurai of old Japan and martial artists of today to Zen. The most eloquent dressage masters have a common thread: their complete disdain for force. It is as if out of the roots of violence, subjugation and war, these few people seek harmony with nature. They try to create something ephemeral. It is art they can never finish. It is art that can't stand still. It is art that is alive. Art that must be watered and fed. In the last analysis it is really the art of living.

My own apprenticeship was no less subtle than the monk's encounter on the bridge. However, more often than not I was not the monk coming home full of balance from the lessons of a wise Rinzai; I was the monk being thrown off the bridge. I still don't know how deep is the river of Zen, but I know precisely how deep, dark and cold is the river water beneath that bridge, having been in it so many times. My apprenticeship covered about thirteen years. It involved traversing thousands of miles. It entailed thousands of hours of rigorous practice. It meant researching centuries of literature penned by old masters, and hours and hours of observation and lectures from new masters. Most of the time it was at the least puzzling, and sometimes it induced such mental upheaval that it pushed my personal life through vast changes. Yet, however much physical time and space I covered, I never even came close to the distance that it was necessary to traverse within the confines of the small sand rectangle, the perfect sand Zen garden, the dressage arena.

Prologue

I AM IN THE dojo of Shuji Maruyama. Mr Maruyama is a disciple of Uyeshiba, the legendary martial artist and founder of Aikido, and a student of Koichi Tohei, founder of the Ki-Aikido Society. Aikido, 'the gentle way', is an odd martial art. It has no offensive moves. It is an incredible awareness and balance. It will use the force of an opponent, move with it, guide it into a turn, or a spin, divert it with a psychic kind of timing until the attack is neutralised. Aikido is grace.

That *Ki* is in the centre of the word Aikido is not an

accident. This Japanese word for 'life force', or 'energy', is the blood of Aikido. In the human being it is centred in the 'hara' – a point below the navel. The closest western term is 'centre of gravity', but this is not a good equivalent. 'Centre of balance' might be better, as long as one does not limit it to physical balance.

I had been using *ki* breathing exercises for my riding for some years. I decided that Aikido could certainly enhance a rider's skills; after all, the dressage rider must train a horse ten times his or her own weight. Force is out of the question. Since I was already using some tenets of Aikido, I thought some more formal instruction would help. This was the second time I had come to Maruyama's training hall. In the evenings, after my riding and training, I had been working in several different dojos. Few were familiar with Aikido and most had drifted far away from the total balance that is at the heart of all martial arts. Maruyama's practice hall was different. It is close to Chinatown in Philadelphia, on the second floor of what looks like a narrow store front. One small door with a few pasted posters marks the entrance. This building is surrounded by short, once useful buildings, all similar. They seem to be held up as much by plywood windows and iron security bars as by bricks and plaster. On street level there are supply rooms, liquor stores, or empty spaces. People cluster on street corners. It has the look of a village at a remote outpost; the order of certain needs is clear.

At the top of a steep flight of stairs is a long, narrow room. There is a modest-sized office, then a small sitting area in front of the mats which go wall to wall to the far end of the room. The sitting area has a few chairs for visitors and a small table that is an unpretentious shrine. Maruyama was gone. He had returned to Japan with his family after sixteen years in America. He did return periodically, but his students, some of whom had been with him for the sixteen years, now run the hall. In front of the mats there is a row of shoes belonging to the people practising.

I have come to watch the practice again and to talk to one of the teachers. It is at least a sixty-mile round trip from my home, and this on top of my horse work. I am not sure that I can manage to attend three or more evenings a week. A woman is going to run the practice. As a few people warm up she walks alone to the back wall of the room. From a simple rack she chooses a bamboo sword and begins some slow movements which have their basis in *kendo*, swordsmastership. She is dressed in the traditional black skirt of advanced Aikido-ists and a white, heavy cotton, robe-like blouse, similar to those worn in other martial arts. She stands deep into the mat. It is easy to move her form five hundred years back in time to the Samurai in Japan. Her hair is like black glass. All her movements seem unhurried. They are smooth, uninhibited; so smooth at times they are very fast. Finally she changes her stance and brings the sword down from above her head in a quick slicing arc. It stops at waist level. For a moment it is still. She has met a certain spot. It has stopped without being abrupt. She returns the sword above her head and two more times she splits the air. Her movements don't seem threatening but there is no confusing what is in front of you. It is serious and commanding.

After the practice she comes over and sits down so that we can talk. She is gracious. She answers my questions. I tell her how impressed I am, but she is very humble. She is straightforward and serene. It is not my imagination. It is peaceful to talk to her. She frequently smiles. I tell her about my ideas of Aikido and riding. She seems ambivalent. At first I think that she is sceptical. Then I realise that she is really listening. She simply doesn't want to make any presumptions. The more we talk, I see that she seems genuinely curious about riding. She almost suggests that she is envious of those who ride horses and live in the country. I assure her I am the envious one. Again she seems embrarrassed. As we continue talking something strange begins to happen. My talk about riding is coming very close to her talk about her own practice. One statement resonates with another, the way a tuning fork can agree with a pure note. There seems little else to say. Sometimes we just nod. A familiar feeling begins to grow inside me. This time I know what is happening. It comes on as a wave of melancholy. I know my apprenticeship is finishing. It is as if someone close to you has died. You are beyond shock and anger. You cannot arouse any more passion. You don't seem to care. The universe is pulling away. You are not sure whether to go on with it, but if you do you know it will be with far fewer expectations. Your ride becomes less ponderous. Since there seems to be less of yourself now; you are automatically less self-important. You are lighter. There is more room. You feel free.

I literally feel myself cracking. Deep in the primitive part of my brain there must be some memory, some programme of metamorphosis from ancient animals. The melancholy, the form with which I have become so familiar, certain that it was my only real self, is disintegrating around me. It is not fighting to hold on. It seems to know better than I do that it is finished. It has been the protective cocoon, until this new transmission, this new form, was possible. How do I know the time is right? What is it in this meeting that sets this off? Before I can try to explain, try to make the right sense of it, I have to go back to the beginning of my serious riding, to what I consider the start of my apprenticeship in the art of dressage. If there was such a thing as a moment of fertilisation or conception in a course of my training, I know for me very well when it was. That is where I have to start.

Chapter One

The Seat

'PULLING THE CHIN IN slightly or making the back of the neck touch the collar will cause the sternum to come forward. This will produce a slight arching of the chest with the deep breathing that promotes posture and relaxation without a bad effect on the position of the other parts of the body . . . The position of the seat bones, as the base of support, vertically underneath the hips and the straight but supple spinal column enables the rider to protect himself against continual contraction of the muscles in the small of his back and his buttocks. It also protects him against fatigue because the point of support lies in the same vertical line as the rider's centre of gravity and he requires no effort to maintain his equilibrium . . .'

Waldemar Seunig[1]

'What is the essence of *zazen*?[2] Just posture, breathing and attitude of mind. In time, every gesture of life becomes zen, but the source, the origin, is simply sitting. The zazen posture is the 'right sitting' . . . Body – the trunk is straight. The pelvis tips slightly forward so the internal organs are placed naturally and the abdomen without tension . . . The head is straight, the chin drawn in . . . Push the sky with your head, push the earth with your knees. The elbows are not glued to the sides, but slightly rounded while the shoulders and arms fall naturally.'

Taisen Deshimaru[3]

A long creek flows in and out of high shale cliffs, along small beaches of grey sand and gravel. In some places the gorges are over one hundred feet deep. This old creek moves through the Tuscarora Indian Reservation on its way into one of the Great Lakes. A brown, smooth farm road follows the creek for half a mile before the water turns hard into one of the high shale

1 SEUNIG, WALDEMAR, *Horsemanship*, Doubleday and Company Inc.
2 *zazen* – the practice of sitting meditating in Zen.
3 DESHIMARU, TAISEN, *The Zen Way to the Martial Arts*, E.P. Dutton, Inc. 1982.

banks, spinning off into the dark shade as the road trails off into a rugged stand of pine trees.

It was on that dirt road bordering the creek and a fertile corn field that my first real introduction to the seat took place. A couple of days before, in a library, I had found a copy of a book on dressage by an Englishman, Henry Wynmalen. I had already been riding for a number of years, both in the American Western style and the English hunt style adapted by Frederico Caprilli, the Italian founder of the forward seat. Wynmalen's book fascinated me. He described the possibility of sitting on a horse in a way that a rider could follow every movement and be practically glued to the horse without relying on grip. I was mesmerised. No one had ever told me anything about this kind of riding. It seemed mystical. The descriptions of the horse's various movements were incredible.

I took Wynmalen's book and one of the two horses that my family owned at the time and went off to the road. It was a clear day. I had a flat, smooth English saddle, a typical old hunting type, with no padding beneath the skirt and built on a tree of a very flat contour. It felt like I was sitting on a wooden plank. I took the stirrups off and began to walk, then trot. The horse seemed to be trotting too fast and I kept sliding from one side to the other. Even though the road was perfectly straight, I could not keep my balance. Time after time I would slip so far over that I had to grab the horse's mane and pull myself up straight.

The horse became nervous from all my wrestling and clutching. We continued in this fashion up and down the road, again and again. The sun fired overhead as the trail of our dust rose above us. Up and then down again. Whenever my legs shook uncontrollably from exhaustion, I would stop and re-read Wynmalen, searching for a clue in the writing, and then I would try again. My legs were rubbed raw and began to bleed. I kept at it. I became angry with myself, but still I continued until complete frustration took over. Finally, it was no use. It was too painful. When I had started at least I could stay on for a little while; now I was falling off every few strides. I had to stop. I was furious with Wynmalen. I looked at the black and white photographs of this frail-looking old man sitting to the trot. I thought it was a hoax. Exaggeration, rotten exaggeration. This old man beyond his prime, sitting there giving us fictitious images. Yet even when my rage with Wynmalen was at its highest, I knew one thing: somehow, deep inside, I felt (although I didn't even have one microscopic piece of evidence) that Wynmalen wasn't a liar. Somehow the old master had set the hook. I told myself that whatever it took, I would get this 'seat' thing. I would master it.

It is midnight and there is an early autumn storm in southern Pennsylvania. The rain is solid and feels even colder because we are leaving Pennsylvania and what has been, for my new wife and me, our first home together as well as our horse business. The lights of the stable reflect in prisms of moisture in the driveway. Our horses are loaded on the lorry. The motor is running. Occasionally they stamp a little nervously. There is the immediate pressure to get going. One of our best friends is there to help. It seems sad to leave. Why I don't have more doubts about this move, I am not sure. The dogs are crated in the car which my wife will drive. If all goes well, sometime in the next day we will arrive at our destination, a piece of land we have bought in the Adirondack Mountains. It is raining harder. There is nothing more to do. We have to go.

The Seat

At college I studied horse management as part of a pre-veterinary course, and in the riding school rode as part of an equitation programme. In the summers I gained more horse experience by working on various farms. After I graduated I tried to work with as many different types of horse as I could – carriage horses, polo ponies, hunters, and at racehorse studs, and event and dressage stables. The girl I married was also involved with horses. We worked together and eventually rented a stable and started our own business. I began teaching. We also both exercised and trained horses. If I could find good dressage instructors, then I tried to have lessons, but they were rare and expensive. I read everything I could find about horsemanship and dressage. By this time I had spent so many hours practising riding without stirrups that the seat seemed much less foreign to me. However, I kept at it. I wasn't anywhere near satisfied even though I could now stay on some difficult horses.

My wife and I worked hard and things began to improve. I was lecturing on horsemanship at a local college and teaching twenty to thirty hours of private lessons during the week. This left less and less time for my own riding. I couldn't believe it – here I was, running my own horse business, something I had always wanted so badly, but it could just as easily be *any* business. It was always business.

Years before, in college, I had hunted up in the Adirondack Mountains with a friend. I loved those mountains. My friend lived there so I asked him to look for a piece of land. One day in the winter, he called me. He had found a perfect place, and it was cheap. I went to see it and bought it. I thought we could start again, small, reshape the business – and ride. I didn't want to teach. I had too much to study. I just wanted to ride all of the time.

As I started to drive away from the Pennsylvania stable I wasn't sure if I would ever see this great horse country again. We survived the night with no breakdowns and I was convinced this was a good omen. In mid-morning, our little caravan drove through the small village of Ironville, where less than fifty people lived. It was still a couple of miles to the farm. The air here was so much drier, and in every direction we could see the peaks of mountains. I was excited. Finally we arrived. We turned the horses out into a wire-fenced paddock. They moved off a little unsteadily into the knee-deep grass. The other pastureland would still have to be reclaimed and permanently fenced. There was not even a barn. The house was falling into two feet of water in the basement. I had cut some trees on a previous visit. They were trucked and milled; now a fresh pile of lumber lay stacked in the dooryard. It would only take me time. I looked at my wife. I wasn't sure what she was feeling.

The stallions scream, partly in defiance, partly in fear. We are having breakfast and looking through the glass doors that face the southern slope of our mountain. From the dressage arena, bordered with white birch rails, the paddocks and pastures divide along the small brook, and run one third of the mountain to the end of the higher timber. There isn't any real cause for alarm. A black bear lumbers through the corner of one of the stallions' paddocks. He is certainly much more afraid of the huge horses. At this time of the day, deer and coyote can often be seen in the higher pastures.

Six years have passed since the move north and that long haul. They have been difficult years, marked by one drama after another. The new barn roof collapsed under a tremendous snow. Water froze for weeks at a time during the long, long winters. Our old house burned down in the middle of a winter's night. Everything was destroyed. We escaped with only the clothes we could carry. All my horse books were ashes. I injured my legs, pinned under a tree in a logging accident. Yet after each disaster we rebuilt and the farm improved. Horses were sent to us to be trained from all over. Our biggest customer was an independent breeder of German Trakehners. We broke many of the young horses and showed the stallions, even though I really didn't like it. I felt it was an interruption and, worse, I didn't like the attitude one seemed to need to be competitive. Through the work with the German horses I was privileged to meet and learn from many good German horsemen, and a couple of bad ones, and for an American at that time, it was an incredible experience. Even though we were reclusive it was a fact that on many given days during that time I probably had the chance to ride more German stallions than most other riders in America. No one then, though, I think could have foreseen the dramatic sweep that the German breeds would make across the USA in a period of a few short years. I read many more German texts and reviewed the popular German riding magazines every month. I pored over the riders of the past and those current. The forms of Loerke, Stensback, Staeck were as familiar to me as the forms of the ever-rising Reiner Klimke and Harry Boldt. With protractor and ruler, I dissected all these riders. I measured the angles of each one's knees and their backs. I calculated the seat in every fashion and matched it to the riders of the Spanish Riding School. Then, in my own practice, I had photographs taken and I compared myself. No master would have pushed me as I did myself. I seemed to be making progress. In spite of many flaws in posture, my seat was becoming more and more effective, more influential and more demanding. When a particular horse went badly, I thought about it all evening. I wouldn't be able to get it out of my mind until I rode that horse again the next day. There were times when I rode the same horse twice. I was riding many hours, sometimes on very difficult horses. I loved working with young horses the most. I took some pleasure in the risk as well as the mystery of each one's potential.

My first wife and I did everything ourselves. The difficulty of the work forced me into equally difficult places with my personality. In order to accomplish the tasks, I needed a forceful intensity. This fierce energy was my ally, but it was hard to shut it off once I got it wound up. One typical day in one of the early winters, there was a problem with a valve at the bottom of a well which was about four feet deep and three feet wide. I had to get to the bottom in order to dismantle and repair it. It was below zero. There was no other way than to take off my coats and shirts, crack the ice on top and reach down, head first, into the icy water. I could not get myself to do these things with nonchalance. I would rev up the fire and bend any task to my will. The danger was that my will seemed to become ravenous once it tasted its own strength. It tried to control everything. With each success it became harder to control. My seat manifested this exact same force. Encounter resistance, strike it down. My seat was becoming more and more a weapon, and it began to concern me.

Sometime in this period, in all my calculations, I had convinced myself that my leg angle was wrong. I lengthened the stirrups as far as possible. This lengthened my leg and gave me the longer, elegant look that I wanted to see. It also tipped my pelvis forward as my thigh fell almost straight down. That this position was uncomfortable to me meant nothing. That it began to pull on the ligaments high up on the inside of my leg was simply the price I would have to pay. After all, I thought, many of the German riders were riding so long they pointed their toes below their heels. The great Theodorescu on his fine mare Cleopatra had his toes lower in almost every photograph. I was riding and training a horse that was closely related to her, a fact which enhanced the theorem. I spent two years stretching my legs until one day I realised I had trained myself into the perfect crotch seat. This is a fault that almost every single dressage book warns against. Yet only when the pain became debilitating did it occur to me that I was sitting badly. Finally, I raised the stirrups with relief. It took the better part of eighteen months for that ligament and muscle to heal to the point where I didn't feel it pull when I mounted a horse. My heels then dropped naturally; my back was released from constant torque and became flexible again. Previously, when I attempted to move my whole leg back further, I tipped my pelvis and arched the small of my back in a tight bow. Now it was easy to keep my leg under my body and my seat bones. I was more patient because I wasn't in pain and my aids were technically more accurate because they were freer.

During these years, I met a riding teacher who would probably have more influence on me than any other I would meet. I was working on a jumping book with a well-known horse photographer, Karl Leck. I sought the help of Dr Henri Van Schaik, who had won a silver medal in the 1936 Olympic Games in Berlin as a member of the Dutch jumping team, and who was now noted as a dressage teacher. I felt that he was a natural to review my writing. I sent him the work. He helped me and we became friends. Whenever possible I tried to have a lesson from him, but it was a five-hour trip to his home. I wrote to him, visited him and watched him teach as often as I could.

In the seat Van Schaik was masterful. A student will sit correctly, no matter how long it takes. If this means you can only walk a horse, so be it. Time seems to mean nothing to him and the student will not move on until the seat is right. To someone in a hurry, he will seem to be an enemy, and will drive him crazy. It was probably through Van Schaik's words and example that I began to put the brakes on my driving aids. He hated the term bracing the back'. He felt it was a poor translation of the correct position of the back even when it is being used as a driving aid. Yet it would take more time before I really knew what he was talking about. Maybe if I could have worked with him more . . . but probably the time was not right yet.

After around seven years in the Adirondack Mountains, my marriage dissolved and the business had to be divided. I stayed on alone to sell the farm. It was the only equitable solution. I needed time to think and readjust. I thought this break should be total, so, for the first time in all those years, I stopped riding. The horses were sold. I began logging for a friend of mine. I spent all day alone in the woods; sometimes I would see another person at lunchtime, just as often I would not.

Spring came, and then the summer. In the evenings I often ate my dinner at a table I had set up under a great old spruce tree facing the mountain that was now for sale. I mowed the empty pastures. Yet I was never lonely. All that time spent alone was important. When I wanted to be around people, I could go to them.

A strange thing was happening. The more proficient I became at my logging work and the more time lapsed since I had stopped riding, the more I thought about it. That summer was spectacular.

I worked for several more months in the autumn. I hunted a lot but I felt my sabbatical was ending. By Christmas I prepared to leave. I arranged everything with the estate agents and within a month I was riding again in Pennsylvania. The farm would be sold shortly afterwards.

On my way back to Pennsylvania, some cosmic cycle completing, I dropped in on an old friend who is an artist. She talked me into visiting a psychic she knew, a woman who was well known and respected by police departments and the like, for her special abilities. In the dark we pulled up at the woman's house in a rural community of upstate New York. The house was so ordinary that I felt comfortable. Before my arrival I had given her my first name and the time of my birth. When we walked in, she handed me a piece of paper. It stated my weight and height. She smiled as she told me that this was just for fun. When we sat down she became more serious.

She began by telling me that I was born under a triune of fire. I listened carefully – this is not something you take lightly when you have narrowly escaped your own death in a fire. Her insights went some way to explaining why I was never really afraid during that raging fire. I clearly remember looking at the charred remains the next morning, being totally possessionless. I felt free. This was a strong lesson in materialism. It is difficult to place too much stock in material goods once you have been shown so dramatically the temporary nature of things.

She talked for two and a half hours without a rest.

There were fascinating connections with riding. She told it all very factually. Finally she had an important story to relate. She told me of a group of Frenchmen who had formed a secret club. They used to design and build escape-proof traps for humans. Then they would put themselves inside these traps and secure them. They had decided that if the human intellect could invent a trap, then the human intellect could also invent an escape. They loved to place themselves in untenable situations and try to find ways out, just for the bizarre challenge of it. Although there was no emphasis in her voice, I couldn't seem to pass over the implication or the advice that seemed so obvious: that the biggest challenges we face are almost always self-made. The escape, therefore, must not be from the trap but from the dangerous process of building the trap for yourself.

The horse's steps are muffled in the soft footing of the indoor arena. The summer sunlight comes through one long open wall that frames a small valley banked by trees and meadow grass. The arena is set in a deep cut between two Pennsylvania ridges. Deer and fox often wander by. The arena is large and usually I have it to myself. I am riding the third horse of the day. This horse is stiff and quietly resistant. I am preparing it for competition for its owner. I ride the horse demandingly. It is now over ten years since I began riding full-time. I push the horse on. The day gets warmer. The horse is reluctant. I ask for more flexibility, for more action behind. My seat drops. I flick the spurs into the horse's flank a couple of times. No noticeable reaction. Some horses become ticklish from the prodding and will actually tighten their sides, freezing some of the motion instead of giving more. I know all these things.

I use more seat. In half an hour I'm wet. The horse

is getting wetter. I drive the horse on. If I get any yielding I hold it and ask for more. More determination, more resistance. We continue around the arena. A spectator might not even be aware that anything out of the ordinary is going on. We work through relatively simple movements, but without rest. I tap the horse with the whip again. I push on through lateral exercises hoping to loosen it, wishing it would give in. I sink my seat even further. I use my back for leverage. Van Schaik would be cringing. I attack a few times with the spurs. I know it is getting aggravating for both of us, yet in terms of technique there is even more I can do to pressurise the horse. I use more strength.

We turn through the corner and are moving straight along the long wall. I ask for more collection. I shorten the horse forcefully. In an instant, the situation explodes. As if in slow motion, like a great marlin breaking high out of the sea to free itself from the fisherman's hook, my horse rises before me. Straight up, straining, slowly shaking its head, twisting in desperate rebellion to free itself of the relentless force on top. The rise goes beyond the highest point and the horse begins to come over, out of balance. Like a great fish, it is falling backwards to the surface. All the horse is in front of me. There is no escape. We keep falling. As we hit the ground there is a horrible sound. The ground is unforgiving. I hear the horse exhale in a deep, full cough. Dust curls up everywhere around us. Enveloped in it, everything becomes still, fog-like. I am lying pinned against the wall of the arena. I have been spared. The horse lies there still and has missed crushing me by inches. Only my leg is trapped. I can see that the horse is alive, conscious. I am not frightened. I am not angry. The situation becomes liquid. I feel as though I am divided – one part of me is looking down at the scene from above. There is disgust and pity. I almost wish I were hurt.

The horse rises to its feet. It seems uninjured. I stand up too. I feel fine, and yet something momentous is building. Horses have reared with me many times. By now I have broken probably fifty to a hundred horses. There have been countless falls. However, before I was always trying to avoid them if they happened. They seemed to be accidents. This time I seem to have deliberately used all my skills and techniques for destruction. What was I doing? My feelings seemed to be bouncing between my different selves. Then, in an amazing process, it became clear to me what the seat was really all about. The Buddhists call it *satori*, an enlightenment, often set off by a dramatic incident. Like some struck monk, after ten years of deliberation, in the violence of the action, I see it all so clearly. Have I become this monster? Have I learned this skill to dominate, to force a proud animal into such anxiety? I look carefully at myself. I am wearing sharp spurs. My horse has whip marks on its flank. I take the spurs off quite calmly. I know that I will never use them again. I can see that I have to go back to the first day of my experience with the seat – that day, along the creek, with Wynmalen's book. Everything was wrong from the moment I gave the concept life. I had promised myself that I would master the seat and nothing had changed since then. I started out by trying to find Wynmalen's seat, then Podhajsky's and Seunig's, obsessively calibrating the seats of the new German riders. From that first day I had a goal, a target. I pushed it in every direction to give me the answer. I created a din of ambition. Increased skill brought me no closer to the truth of the situation. In fact, my dominating seat became a wedge, separating me from what I really wanted. My seat became insular and demanding in that it took on a life of its own. When you are talking all the time, issuing orders, you cannot hear. Never did I just listen. Never did I just sit and feel for myself what was going on. Hear the horse. In the absence of language and words, the natural world speaks in whispered feelings. I had to go back to the beginning. In the mind of the beginner, all things are possible. In the mind of the expert, few.

The quotes at the beginning of this chapter come from very diverse sources. They are worlds apart in culture, and in time. Yet their languages are almost identical, and there are many other examples. I do not believe this is coincidental. There are no coincidences in the postures of the seat – riding, *zazen*, martial arts. Posture is all-encompassing. Breathing is a path, and awareness is the result. If we inhibit awareness through contortions of the body or contortions of the mind, the results will be the same: a rigid being and, in riding, an inflexible seat. The correct posture alone has the power to open one's consciousness.

In the beginning I think it is important to concentrate on breathing. Not because breathing has magical powers of its own, but because it gives the mind something natural to do, without focussing its attention on conceptualisation, or too much thinking. It is well known in sorcery that if you want to manipulate someone, you need to control his attention. It doesn't matter if the subject's attention is centred on the sorcerer out of admiration, hanging on every word, or out of sheer hate or fear. Once the subject is occupied, the sorcerer can manipulate him at will. Breathing can free misguided attention – and to breathe well, you must have good posture. Furthermore only in an aware posture will you be receptive to the murmurs outside of yourself. If you are uncomfortable and tense, you cannot feel. After all, riding is feeling.

It is now my belief that a rider, properly positioned by a good teacher, can feel 'the correct seat' in his very first riding lesson. It might be, in fact it most probably will be, only for a fraction of a second in a whole hour's practice. How hard you try doesn't really matter. It may happen by accident. If the teacher adjusts and the rider allows himself to just be aware, the feeling will come back. Like a shy and curious cat, if you make a move for it, force yourself on it, it is gone. If you just sit quietly and wait, then sooner or later it will come sneaking back.

The horse will want to communicate with you through your seat. However, this is precisely the dilemma. Too many of us think we have so many important things to say, that the ego will not quieten down.

Imagine finding a great radio, call it Ego's Radio. It has channels to and from all parts of the world. You turn it on, and as you slowly turn through the dial mysterious and musical sounds of foreign dialects come out from all over the world. If you wish, you can begin the long, arduous study of these languages. The result may be that you will be able to truly communicate with these strange exotic people and learn things you may have thought were never possible. You may learn new perceptions and share different visions of life. Or you can turn one switch and broadcast – send your own messages out and leave it to others to learn to understand you if they so want.

In the world of riding, you will very quickly meet up with Ego's Radio. You must decide for yourself whether to listen or speak.

What I have learned is that the correct seat is never only a matter of the physique or its physical properties, even though they are essential. Many riders, even very skilful riders, never leave this plane.

However, if you study the seat *mushotoku* (the Japanese word meaning without desire for gain or profit), you can move towards a new plane that is much more profound: a way of perceiving, of being, of feeling part of and connected to the whole world outside yourself. With the right practice, the right concentration will develop, until you can hold yourself in balance on the horse, aware, in full power, without tension. This is the fundament of the seat – that it is a way of perceiving as well as influencing. The shy cat sits purring in your lap. The world of the horse begins to reveal itself to you, just by your sitting there correctly. The doors open. You are accepted, not tolerated. After that, nothing about the human world can be the same again.

Chapter Two

The Hands – The Longitudinal Field of Balance

IN HIS BOOK *Piaffer and Passage*[1] Colonel Decarpentry says about balancing the horse, 'never increase the pressure of the hands and legs at the same time'. In *The Complete Training of the Horse and Rider*[2] Alois

[1] DECARPENTRY, COLONEL, *Piaffer and Passage*, Arco Publishing Co., 1975.
[2] PODHAJSKY, ALOIS, *The Complete Training of the Horse and Rider in the Principles of Classic Horsemanship*, Wiltshire Book Co., 1967.

Podhajsky, writing on exactly the same topic, says, 'short action [of the reins] must be supported by the rider's legs pushing forward'.

Classical riding theory abounds with these apparent contradictions. The student of equitation must face them like quintessential Zen *koan*[3] riddles. The student interested only in the end result is in a terrible position. A wrong turn towards either master may ruin months of precious time spent training the horse. The student interested in the path or process is in a fascinating position. He may step into a new place, perhaps a place where Podhajsky or Decarpentry has never been. No matter where this student ends up, he will be happy for the chance to travel there on the back of a horse.

What Decarpentry and Podhajsky are talking about, of course, is the half-halt. A look at the half-halt may be a good way to look at the rider's hands. In a dull night sky you can often see the light of stars by not looking directly at them. The corners of your eyes are better at detecting this kind of light. Without harsh, direct scrutiny, the stars will reveal themselves.

The New England air is cool. The hills are green, but they are beginning to show small breaks of reds and rust colours. I have brought one of the young stallions to a horse trials competition. I feel a certain pressure. The owners of the horse will be there and several people who have mares to breed from will be watching him. He is still green in terms of performance. He has also been learning about his role as a stallion and sometimes it is difficult to control his libido. Still, I feel that he needs to be taken out in public. I want him to see other horses in a situation unconnected with breeding. If he

[3] Apparent dichotomies or paradoxes used as a system of meditative study to deepen a student's understanding.

can understand the difference, it will be easier to control him for the rest of his life.

After the dressage test, he is in second place. His performance was all right. He is aware of all the other horses and very curious about the mares. None, I hope, are in season. I keep him busy.

The cross-country phase is next. After walking the course I see no particular problems. In a few vantage points spectators are gathering; in fact, there are more people than he has ever seen before. In between fences I will try to ride him towards the crowd to make sure that he sees them and becomes familiar with their movement. Our time comes up. We are counted down in the starter's box, and we gallop off. At the second fence he raps his front legs hard on the obstacle, and wobbles on landing. In a way I am glad. I feel it may make him more alert on the remainder of the course. Just to make sure he understands that I'm not too happy, I tap him with the stick I'm carrying. Later on in the course I feel him lag in the middle of a combination. I use the stick hard, once, and he responds. He pulls me over the second element of the obstacle. It is fine; he feels aggressive and I would much rather have that kind of feeling. At the end he is clear and has made it under the time without really trying. After the scores are added up and recalibrated, he moves into first place.

The last phase is the show-jumping test. Unlike cross-country fences, which are solid and unyielding, show jumps will fall if struck; and each rail can cost penalty points. The day has dragged on. The competition is friendly and the organisation leisurely, but it is getting late. In this last phase the competitors jump in reverse order. Being first, we must go last. By the time we enter the arena it has clouded over. It is drizzling and near dusk. We begin. After the third fence with nine to go, we start hitting rails. Penalty points add up. The horse seems less and less respectful of the jumps, dragging his feet as he leaves the ground. By the time we cross the finish flags we have dropped back six or seven places. I am tired and disappointed. I contain my feelings. Everyone blames it on the light. I put it down to his inexperience but I know we have a problem. It is a long ride home. Over the hours, I go over the round again and again in my mind. Every bad move is painfully vivid. I can't seem to come up with an answer. I am baffled. I am not sure that I rode badly, but I am certain that I didn't have have him trained well enough. I run through more remedies trying to find some way to get him to start picking his front feet up. I wear myself out rethinking everything too far ahead.

A month has passed since the horse's competition. It is cooling off more. I am aware of winter approaching. There isn't much more time in this season to work outside. I have been schooling and schooling but I am getting nowhere. In a course of ten fences we still knock down three rails at least. If this problem is not solved, the horse will beat himself at every competition and, what is worse, may pick up a reputation as a bad jumper, which will limit his value as a breeding stallion. I know that many other trainers would adopt extreme measures of punishment for this apparent lack of concentration, making it decidedly painful for him to touch the rails anywhere. I am opposed to these measures. Somehow I feel they can't solve my problem, which is not only to correct the horse but to understand what is going on. Each day my frustration increases. I feel time is running out literally. I dread going into the winter without a solution.

On one particular day I begin my practice with this horse. The sun has softened the footing. The old turf is firm but spongey, perfect to jump on. He is the second horse of the morning. I start patiently. I try to ride him lightly and freely. After the warm-up we begin working through some jumping grids, combinations of fences aimed at increasing the horse's dexterity. After a little while he seems to stop trying. It feels as if he is deliberately reaching out to knock down the rails. I am thinking as fast as I can, when all of a sudden my will takes over. I see a solid cross-country fence. This part of me seems to have had enough. I start cantering towards the fence. About ten strides from the fence I feel the horse lag a little. He trips forward, trying to brake for the fence. I take the reins in one hand and strike him hard with the crop. At the same time I sit down in the saddle. I am upright, almost in a dressage seat. I close my legs hard, press the spurs to the horse's sides. In the back of my mind I have a fleeting image of an explosion at the fence like some crashing racing car, an elemental chassis careening forward as pieces fly off, trailing smoke and fire. Yet it doesn't have any effect on my body. My determination fails to heed the warning from my intellect. I drive the horse ever harder. The horse scrambles a little, but miraculously yanks his front feet up in time, even at that speed. I can't believe it. I ride on to another fence without stopping. Ten strides out I begin driving again. We are flying. This time he stands back and sails. I take him into five more fences. The harder I try to push him into the fence, the better he jumps. I go back to the arena and jump five fences clean. I stop and settle. I am mystified. My mind is quiet, almost sheepish. It isn't raging with questions or solutions – it is speechless. I feel ambivalent. My will and mind seem to be at cross-purposes, one subjugating the other. There is a paradox here. When my intellect is ruling, it seems deliberately to try to obstruct my will.

If it is left unchecked, it can increase the tension around me and inside me to such an extent that it freezes my body and prevents it from functioning. The idea of ferociously thinking up solutions stops me from finding one. When my will takes over, it couldn't care less about danger. To my mind this seems excessive and hazardous. My mind is fearful of my will, believing that it will always put me in very dangerous places. Yet at the times when I have faced my own death, the facts do not support this. When my house was on fire and a silent pall of black smoke was descending upon me, my intellect was calmly sleeping. It was some other part of me that perceived the danger and woke me a few minutes before I was smothered. Wasn't it my intellect and ambition that chose those paths which backed me into corners, where only a sheer burst of will could free me from the destructive tangle of my ideas? At those times when my will seemed excessive and irrational, whose fault was it really?

I wonder if I can ever merge the two or if they will ever do it themselves? It is troubling that as carefully as I think a problem through, I never seem to solve it until my will takes over. I can see very easily how successes can become connected with the force of will. I am leery of this connection between success and force. If it turns out that I become less interested in force, will it mean less interest in successes? Or will a new idea of success come into being?

I am also mystified because I know I have stumbled on to something important. It is fairly easy to explain physically what has happened. Intellectually one can describe some relatively simple physical laws. The thrust on the accelerator of a racing car shifts the car's weight over the rear driving tyres. The front end lightens with this transfer. You can flip a motorcycle over with a similar burst of power. Isn't it the same with this horse? Maybe. But there is so much more.

A human being is fairly vertically oriented in terms of balance. The human's centre of balance is pretty well determined and set. We are keenly aware of this balance. It takes us a long time after we are born to accomplish the feat of standing and moving upright in balance. Almost all other animals move at birth in the same way that they will move as adults. Not humans. It is difficult to move upright over only two legs. The horse's centre of balance has a whole range along its longitudinal axis, which could roughly correlate to the horse's spine. In various phases of its gaits, its balance, like its weight, can shift from front to rear. When horse and rider join together to move as a team, this new union has a centre of balance that is different from that of either of its members alone.

What I had encountered that was so mystifying was this distinct shift in perception. I had shifted from my two-legged sense of equilibrium and balance to the perception of a four-legged's balance. I had become aware of and able to feel this whole longitudinal field inside which the horse can shift its centre of balance. Before my will took over I kept thinking about balance instead of feeling it. I thought that, to make the forehand lighter, I had to ride lighter and more carefully. The more careful I became, the more rails went down. The more the focus was on what I could do and on myself, the more I pulled us, as a team, off balance. It was only when my intellect and mind were totally frustrated and confused that a crack appeared for my body to take over, to get its chance. What did I have to lose? I was out of ideas. Now there was room for something new. Instead of dictating all the possibilities, I could listen with my whole body. I felt the answer.

Balancing, rebalancing and shifting the horse's centre of balance is the cornerstone of dressage. The half-halt is a technique for getting at the constant rebalancing that goes on with this longitudinal field inside the horse. If it is in the seat that the rider begins to find his own centre of balance and thus awareness, then in the half-halt this awareness will send the rider deeper into the horse, where he will be able to sense something of the horse's centre of balance. Ultimately horse and rider will come to a place where they will merge into something quite new: a place, a feeling, where the rider will literally be at one with the horse.

In true dressage this balancing is the practical reason for doing dressage. This balancing *is* dressage, and not the particular movements in themselves. In the introduction I said that dressage is not necessarily an esoteric ballet-like endeavour, although it can look like one. This is what I meant. You must look at dressage with more than your eyes. Movements executed without balance and transitions between them become simply strings of acrobatic tricks. In true dressage it is the continuum that is important. There is the most pragmatic of all goals in dressage – to help train the horse to learn to balance with the additional weight and mass of the rider on top.

The very best dressage riders become keenly aware of the balance of the horse. They never let the horse fall too far out of balance. This is so critical a feeling that in advanced dressage the rider is asked to prove that he has command over this perception of balance in the course of riding. The correct piaffe, a cadenced trot in place, is nothing more than a manifestation of moving this centre of balance backwards. In a very real sense it can be argued that the piaffe means nothing on its own.

Its whole reason for being is to see how horse and rider can move in the longitudinal field of balance.

Riders who are abrupt, pushing the horse from the legs into the hands, pulling with the hands trying to put the horse back towards the legs, falling in and out of balance during the movements, have to be considered novices to the art of dressage no matter what difficult movements are executed. In dressage it is always how they are executed, not that they are executed.

A great deal of literature concerning the half-halt uses explanations like 'lightening the forehand', 'lifting the head and neck', 'elevating the poll', and 'raising the forequarters'. A logical reading of much of this theory would imply something has to be done to the front end of the horse in order to lighten it. Yet the reality is opposite. Imagine you are sitting astride the centre of a seasaw at a children's playground, and there is a rope tied to the end of the seesaw in front of you, just as reins would go towards the horse's head. As long as you sit on the fulcrum it is easy for the board to move up or down. The board is balanced and you are not impeding it. Now slide forward a little and the board immediately drops in front of you. You are tipped forward, looking towards the ground. The tail of the board is high in the air behind you. You have the rope so why not just pull the board back up? You pull on the rope. You can of course pull on the rope forever. You will never be able to lift that board back off the ground until you move your seat back over the centre of balance. When you do, the board will be as light as a feather.

In true dressage the hands only work at refining the edges, adjusting something that is already relatively in balance. They can never by themselves put the horse back into balance, any more than a person can pull the seesaw back up to an equilibrium if the balance is tipped off centre.

A child walks along a balance beam. The aware coach walks beside her. The child begins to falter. The coach instantly reaches up and steadies the child around the waist, which is close to a human's centre of gravity. As soon as the child is in balance again, the coach releases. They continue. The child's steps become bigger, freer, with each repetition. The child can stay in balance for longer periods of time and eventually through the complexity of new movements.

Good half-halts work this way. The aware rider gives them to try to keep the horse in balance. The most important part of the half-halt is the release. If the driving aids and/or the restraining aids are applied to shift the centre of balance back further, they must be released the split second rebalancing occurs. Those next steps taken by the horse will always be the most beautiful. The balance is readjusted and the horse is freed of any restraints and the steps show this.

Back at the gym, the child turns and begins another pass. An expert gymnast comes into the gym. She begins to limber up. The coach notices her. His concentration lapses. The child before him loses her balance. The coach isn't aware. The child slips and falls off the beam on to the mats. She is unhurt. The coach apologises. He retrains his attention. The child climbs up and begins again. This time her steps are more tentative, short and tense. The child is mildly anxious. She is having a hard time staying on the beam. The coach holds her all the way across. The minute he tries to release, she starts to fall.

Bad half-halts work this way. If the rider lets the horse fall too far out of balance, the results will always be forceful and shocking. This kind of riding causes

[45]

anxiety and a myriad manifestations will start to occur. Tension is insidious in riding. The rider has to do everything to limit it. If the rider can't release even the tense horse, then, like the unnerved gymnast, the horse won't be able to move without some psychological or balancing life-line.

Dressage literature tells the reader to load the haunches of the horse, using the half-halt as a tool to do this. However, it can only do this for a few seconds. If there isn't an immediate release, the horse's action will freeze and become unnatural. The horse will begin to try to lean on the reins for support. From there the hind legs will start pushing the weight forward instead of carrying it forward. If the rider is not fully and constantly aware, he can just as easily train the horse to be heavy and dull as he can to be light and free.

REIN EFFECTS

Many teachings in riding are very specific as to the number of rein effects that there are. Some will say there are five. Sometimes these different effects are clearly described and given names: for example, opening rein, rein of opposition, indirect rein. Furthermore, there has been great debate over whether the reins should be taut and elastic, or soft, loose, and semi-slack.

Why is there so much attention paid to the reins, and therefore the rider's hands, when universally all masters agree that the real controlling is done at the true source of power in the horse, namely the rear or hind end, and that excessive rein use will be harmful?

One obvious answer is that the young mounted horse does not instantly appear in balance. Like the child on our balance beam, the young horse will fall in and out of balance and will be constantly readjusting its equilibrium along its longitudinal field of balance. The rider can help to rebalance the horse with restraining rein aids: not by pulling the horse back into balance, but by slowing the motion for a split second so that the hind end, in effect, can catch up. It is almost like damming up a river; the power is stored behind the dam. In applying this very brief rein effect, the hand must not pull back to where it would have a braking effect. This would only put the horse further on to its nose, much as when a driver brakes in a car and the bonnet dives down. Instead the hand is passive and poised, 'fixed', for a moment, and the power bunches or pushes up into it. The horse becomes rounder, with its hind legs up further under its body, and rebalancing occurs. Again, the moment this happens, the rider must free the horse once more.

Another answer is that this infatuation with rein effects is a man-made problem. In terms of my own experience, I began to feel and see an obvious mistake in my riding and training. Early in my dressage instruction and continuing through a lot of it, the term 'forward' was drilled into my riding style. It is an expression of one of the most basic tenets of dressage, and for me one of the most misunderstood. Forward riding has always been described as animated, decisive action in the gaits, impulse in spirit. (The opposite of sluggish, aimless or wandering gaits and movement.) In my attempts to satisfy the desire of judges and teachers to see horses moving more forward, always more forward, invariably I applied too much push or thrust behind by using too vigorous and too constant leg aids. Because this was coupled with the natural inexperienced timing of an apprentice, I very often pushed my horses on to the forehand instead of seeking an equilibrium over the four legs, or even a little more towards the rear as in the collected paces. The result was always the same. The horse became heavier in my hands and not lighter. It took a very long time to learn to trust my feelings and to wait until the horse had mastered one level of animation before injecting any more impulsion. When I stopped chasing my horses forward, they automatically became lighter. If there wasn't enough movement, so be it. Until the horse could carry what was there, there was no point in pressing on for more.

In terms of the specific numbers of rein effects and their descriptions, I have found reality much different. Basically the hands of the rider can move: (a) in a vertical field parallel to the rider's spine, up and down; and (b) in a horizontal field, parallel to the horse's spine towards the horse's mouth and back towards the rider's torso.

In the three-dimensional space of intersection between these two fields, there is an infinite number of combinations and effects possible, and that is if both reins are applied symmetrically, which they almost never are. Therefore, you have infinity times two when you include unilateral rein aids as well. In my opinion on rein effects, there is only one feeling that really needs to be mastered. It is the feeling of heaviness or lightness. If the reins are becoming heavy, an alarm should be sounding off in the horseman's head, and it should not go off until they become light.

When I first started riding one of the greatest compliments one could hear was that so and so had 'good hands', 'light hands', or 'quiet hands'. It was conversely very bad to have active hands. It is now my feeling that the novice rider should be allowed to move his hands around. This is the only way to develop the dexterity which will eventually translate into educated touch and real finesse. If the novice rider is constantly forced to keep his hands immobile, I believe they can turn into dead hands, with little capacity to feel and even less, to effect. If you take a pen in the hand opposite to that with which you write and you try to sign your name, you immediately become aware of the ineptitude of the one and the practised dexterity of the other. The more practice, the more facile. If you want to see fine, co-ordinated hands, you have to let the novice rider move his hands up and down, forward and back, deliberately encouraging him to move them and not keep them dead still. In this way as dexterity improves, so will feel.

'A lot of riders know inside rein, outside rein, but they do not know how to work all those degrees between nerves and relaxation. . . .'

Nuno Oliveira

Chapter Three

The Legs – The Lateral Field of Balance

'IN HIS USE OF language, La Guerinière was not very disciplined and this provoked misconceptions and

[50]

caused Parocel, his illustrator, to draw the wrong diagrams.'[1]

H. L. M. Van Schaik

'Unlike the writing of his predecessors, his [de la Guerinière's] book is clear and easy to understand. He based it on simplicity and facts in order to be completely understood by his readers.'[2]

Alois Podhajsky

In modern riding few movements or theories about movements have captured as much attention or stirred as much vitriolic argument as the shoulder-in and leg yielding. These two movements are predominately controlled by the rider's legs and have an effect on the horse's legs and body. Since they have been argued by some of the most outstanding horsemen and trainers, I think if we look at these movements something important may be revealed about the use of the rider's legs.

I came across the dilemma of leg yielding and shoulder-in again and again through various literature during my apprenticeship, and more importantly through two riding masters who taught me and who were diametrically opposed on the proper execution of the shoulder-in. Once again no amount of mental gymnastics could free me from the confusion of these two schools of thought, especially since either man could execute perfectly the movement in question. It was only after years

[1] VAN SCHAIK, H. L. M., *Misconceptions and Simple Truths in Dressage*, J. A. Allen, London, 1986.
[2] PODHAJSKY, ALOIS, *The Complete Training of Horse and Rider in the Principles of Classic Horsemanship*, Wiltshire Book Co., 1967.

of my own practice in the dressage arena that I began to feel an answer to this riddle.

We know from reading historical literature that during the time of Pluvinel, trainers used forms of leg yielding. Pluvinel, who invented the use of pillars, used to work a horse around a single pillar in a side-stepping fashion. Pluvinel pushed the horse sideways while its cavesson was attached to the pillar. The horse's spine was relatively straight and both its front and hind legs criss-crossed. The horse performed this kind of circling traverse around Pluvinel and the pillar. Similar work can still be seen today in Portugal but without the aid of a pillar: a trainer stands near the horse's shoulder holding the reins in one hand and with the other pushes the horse sideways with touches of the whip. The horse is worked first one way and then the other. This exercise sensitises the horse to signals of touch on its sides and teaches it early on to move away from even a light touch on its side. This is not totally natural for the horse: often ticklish or belligerent horses will lean against pressure instead of yielding to it. If the horse learns to use its considerable strength against the will and signals of the rider, no rider will ever be able to work with it, since in the end no human rider can overpower a horse ten times his own weight. So these early lessons are very critical psychologically, much more than physically. These movements of leg yielding, either unmounted or mounted, have always been fundamentally loosening, warm-up-type exercises, and they are the first lessons the horse learns about the rider's legs.

In approximately the 1730s François Robichon de la Guerinière was credited with inventing or creating the shoulder-in. This movement could be performed along the wall and looked similar to leg yielding, but with a very important distinction: the horse's body had lateral bend. Its spine was curved deliberately, by pressure from the rider's inside leg. With one side of the horse's body constricted around the rider's leg and one side stretched out along the outside of this curve, this exercise had obvious gymnastic value. Here was an exercise which could attack the one-sidedness with which all horses are born. This one-sidedness is probably some manifestation of a split brain, analogous to right- and left-handedness in humans. The shoulder-in, moving forward and holding a sideways curve at the same time, gained even more gymnastic value by playing off these apparently opposing sets of directions. Finally this enigmatic movement had the ability to rebalance the horse towards collection, which lightened the horse in the hands of the rider.

What happened over a period of time was that two distinct schools of thought grew from the creation of the shoulder-in. One developed into the modern shoulder-in as described by the FEI, which has a strong Germanic tradition. In this movement the haunches are straight and the bend develops from the straight haunches towards the horse's ears. The horse leaves only three imaginary lines of tracks because the inside hind leg and the outside front leg move in the same line. The second school of thought prefers a shoulder-in on four lines of tracks, similar to engravings that accompany la Guerinière's text. It can be seen being practised at many classical riding schools in Europe. In this shoulder-in the horse is also bent along the spine, so it is not like leg yielding, but the haunches are not straight like the modern shoulder-in.

I came first to the shoulder-in under the influence of the Germanic theory, especially put forward by Steinbrecht. My own masterful teacher of the time was in full agreement. It was insisted that this theory and practice was the real essence of la Guerinière's shoulder-in, and my teacher could precisely quote the French script. The essence was the loading of the haunches, especially the loading of the inner hind leg. The haunches had to remain straight with the bend starting approximately at a point in between the horse's hips and curving forward towards the head. The horse would leave three lines of tracks, with the inner hind leg and outer front leg travelling along the same line. It was argued that only this kind of shoulder-in could truly collect the horse and gymnastically enhance it, by virtue of making the inner hind leg step up under the curving body. If the rider let this bend out by releasing the pressure of his outside leg, which was behind the girth and behind his inside leg, the haunches would then turn out. The horse's spine would automatically then straighten out a little and the hind legs would begin to side step. The theory reasoned that if that happens the horse escapes the true loading of the hind legs, which is what develops collection and lightening of the forehand, and the exercise becomes more like leg yielding which was always considered to be a loosening exercise and never a collecting one. When sideways movement takes precedence over forward movement, the driving force[3] exerted by the hind legs is interrupted. In the worst case, a full sideways traverse, the hind end loses almost all power for propulsion.

In this kind of shoulder-in it was always explained that although la Guerinière clearly stated that the hind legs should cross over, he really meant that the legs and feet cross past each other. The engravings that accompany la Guerinière's text do not bear this out

---

[3] George Pratt Jnr's remarks on gait analysis: This driving force depresses the hindquarters and lightens the forehand with torque around the centre of mass of the horse through a very complex series of muscular contractions throughout the whole hind-end system.

because they clearly show four lines of tracks. These engravings were not considered to be definitive because they were not made by la Guerinière himself.

Later in my apprenticeship I had the opportunity to work with another outstanding master who held the opposite opinion. He was convinced that when la Guerinière said that the hind legs should cross over, he meant cross over and not cross by, as they do in every normal stride. He was equally convinced that the engravings were correct and were further proof of the text. The true classic shoulder-in was to be executed on four lines of tracks with bend in and along the spine, but not straight haunches. Furthermore, he always maintained that there is no problem with escaping haunches if the rider is aware.

There they stood in front of me, like the two Japanese swordmasters: neither had a weakness, and yet a loyal student can feel double the weakness for both of them. I continued to study and practise and eventually two curious things happened. One was that I began to feel that the weight of the evidence was against my Germanic teachers concerning their claim of inheritance to the classic shoulder-in of la Guerinière. It simply took too much intellectual reaching to arrive at a straight-haunches, three-track shoulder-in out of la Guerinière's text. He clearly speaks of criss-crossing hind legs as well as bending of the spine. It has been pointed out to me that *chevaler* (in ancient French) is criss-crossing, and that la Guerinière repeatedly speaks of *chevalen* – which is to criss-cross or to straddle with the hind feet, and this simply cannot be ignored. Furthermore, to denounce the engravings as inaccurate would not make sense, since no less an authority than la Guerinière himself endorses them in the preface of his book *Ecole de Cavalerie:*

'Not only did I make a point in giving clear, neat, precise definitions, but in order to make them more comprehensible, I added to this work boards which will ease and lift the difficulties. In those matters, what is exposed to the eyes becomes infinitely more sensible than all what is described – whatever art is used thereto. It is after the originals, and under the direction of M. Parocel, regular painter to the king and his Royal Academy, whose reputation in this genre is generally known, that the different airs of Manège which figure in the second part, were engraved. I also set diagrams in order to show the proportions of terrain that one should observe in the different ways to supple and work the horse.'[4]

The second thing I found happening was that although I felt the four-track shoulder-in was the true classical shoulder-in, I found the three track shoulder-in to be a better gymnastic tool. I began to believe more and more in the superior gymnastic value of the modern shoulder-in. However, I also realised that it is difficult to demand it of a green horse.

As I rode in my practice I saw a recurrent problem in a simple but elegantly difficult exercise. I would ride down the centre line of the arena in shoulder-in and at about the middle I would turn off into an eight- or ten-metre circle. When I returned to the centre line I would continue in the shoulder-in down the remainder of the centre line. It was always at the moment when I returned to the shoulder-in that the exercise faltered. Unless I had a firm outside leg towards the haunches, the haunches would invariably slip out. They would lose their straightness. The horse would begin taking criss-crossing,

[4] *Ecole de Cavalerie*, La Guerinière's preface, as translated by Jean-Claude Racinet.

traverse steps behind. As the horse took sideways steps behind, it would automatically lose the forward driving power that comes most efficiently from straight square haunches. There is a simple inverse relationship between driving force and sideways movement behind. The more sideways, the less drive. This follows true to gait analysis which describes the driving force as depressing the hindquarters and lightening the forehand with torque around the centre of mass of the horse.[5] One can then see why leg yielding would have a deleterious effect on collecting up the horse, and conversely why the modern shoulder-in with its straight haunches would have a distinct physical advantage in working the horse in collection and lightening the forehand. Here, while working in a bend, the trainer tries not to disturb the power thereby training for flexibility and strength.

It seemed true, as Steinbrecht had said, that escaping haunches would drag behind as it were, instead of creating the drive which fosters collection. However, the more I practised this exercise and its variations, the more I realised how difficult it really was to execute. By this time I had trained more than fifty horses to do the shoulder-in and I found it to be impossible for a green horse who had not mastered some collection. Whereas I could do leg yielding from almost the first day in the saddle, there was the rub. It seemed that his modern shoulder-in was as much a verification of collection as a path to collection.

It was during these practices that it became clear to me that leg yielding, la Guerinière's shoulder-in, and the modern shoulder-in were simply a continuum of lateral exercises. Each of my young horses went through

---

[5] George Pratt Jnr's remarks on gait analysis.

all these stages and probably many in between. Some horses progressed quickly, the stiffer ones more slowly.

It also became clear to me that simply forcing the horse into the position of the modern FEI shoulder-in was certainly no guarantee that the horse would be collected. If the horse were pushed too early and forced into the bend, it could become cramped and the hind legs would stiffen and lose all their freedom of reach and drive. So it looked as if Steinbrecht's worst fear of dragging haunches was to become another of those incredible paradoxes. The position of the modern shoulder-in is supposed to ensure collection, and yet if it is assumed too quickly, too early, it can also lead to dragging haunches by restricting the horse's movement.

A further paradox I found was that leg yielding was only supposed to have limited use and effect as a loosening exercise. Yet I found a few steps of leg yielding even at the walk could free a heavy horse from the rider's hands by distracting the horse from its fixation on the reins and bit and transferring its attention to the rider's legs without the added confusion of forward impulse. In these cases it curiously worked like the best collecting exercise in freeing the back of the horse and encouraging it to step lively again.

In the end I found my awareness had to focus on feeling the horse under me. I had to feel when the bending was too much and was killing forward impulse, or when there wasn't enough bend and the horse was just lying on my hands. The rider cannot separate the concept of a lateral exercise from the actual lateral riding, or he will begin to get an image in his mind of what a correct lateral movement should look like. A correct lateral movement is a matter of feeling. What is even worse for those who must pin it down, is that a correct lateral movement may change. Since it is a gymnastic exercise, what is good for the horse one day may not be good enough in a few weeks. The rider has to be careful not to strangle the movement by some conceptualisation which determines forever the exact placement of footfalls or exact angulation.

Finally, how does one account for the vitriolic rebuttal and counter rebuttals that have occurred over the years on this subject? Is it just a matter of racism or nationalism? Certainly one cannot minimise the political trauma that the various national schools of riding underwent, especially when dynamic and flamboyant horsemen appeared and reappeared on the scene. The effect of Baucher, for example, could certainly fill an interesting book. There were also complex cross-overs between individuals belonging to certain so-called national schools. The more modern world alone was responsible for the breakdown of strong regionalisms. Although I have always felt that these were factors, there was something more important under all of this. After all, some of these men were masters of high integrity. Most were careful masters, regardless of the school of thought that was always specific as to how their lateral work should be done. There is universal attention to detail. This attention to detail opens a 'Pandora's box' in terms of opposing viewpoints. Yet both schools of the shoulder-in know very well that if lateral movement in the horse does not have its basis in the rider's seat and legs, then imitation flexibility will come from the rider's hands. These kinds of riders will pull their horse's heads from side to side trying to create some suppleness. This is why I think there is so much attention paid to the detail of lateral work. Every exercise has in it a potential to build but also a potential to destroy if abused or over-used. I believe this is what most knowledgeable masters live in fear of, to see lateral work degenerate into abuse, because the principles behind it have been lost.

If these exercises are used incorrectly they can cause irreparable damage. Today, as in the past, we can see a lot of riders pulling their horse's heads from side to side or riding on circles bent to the outside. There are many variations of these invented exercises. However, there comes a point where they become contraindicative in that as they push a horse against the normal flexion and extension of a joint, they create a tension instead of suppleness. Exercises of counter bends etc., in opposite direction to movement, have an incredible potential for harm. In bending a horse's joints against their normal flexion and extension they create pain, which the horse in turn instantly feels and resists in order to protect itself from hyperextension which could damage ligaments, tendons and even bone. The horse's normal action will be very quickly paralysed, and what some riders feel as increased activity is a circussy stiffening, which will only lead to more stiffening and eventually collapse. Anyone who has ever been in northern woodland after a heavy spring snow has seen beautiful white birch trees bent in unnatural loops, leaning at freakish angles, as a result of being sprung by the inordinately heavy, wet snow load. The plasticity of these trees was pressed beyond a point of recovery. Once matter like this is pressured so severely, either all at once or with frequently repeated smaller overloads, it will weaken to the point where it cannot recover. I am convinced that all knowledgeable masters are familiar with this phenomenon and have seen horses broken past a point of elastic recovery. It is a sad and permanent sight and I believe it is the real motivation behind the attention to detail in lateral work.

In my own experience I have seen some Western horses being trained for pleasure riding in the western

United States. These horses had their heads tied to their hocks with a rope rig in an effort to make them surrender in the neck. They were also subjected to very long shank bits and riders with long split reins pulled their horse's heads from side to side. The result was the total and complete destruction of the horse's natural movement. They were incapable of decisive forward motion in a straight line. They were so rubbery that the bridle and bit had no connection to the back or the haunches. They were ruined like the birch trees. I don't mean to cast aspersions on all Western riders or riding, because I have seen good Western riders and things in so-called dressage practice which rival the abuse of exercise, but it was there that I became so clearly aware of the dangers.

I began to understand the reason for the specific writings of many of the masters and their carefully worded warnings. I was not so much concerned about converting a rider to one school of thought or another, but to convert the rider to any school of thought with a harmonious plan, not any whim or twist. Above all, I now see the great debates on leg yielding, la Guerinière's shoulder-in, and the FEI or modern shoulder-in as allegories, seemingly different but always illuminating the complete disdain of force. They were attempts to speak out, over and over again, that all exercises – and in this case lateral exercise – must work on developing the normal extension and the flexion of a joint or cluster of joints. This will require of the rider a knowledge of anatomy so that he will never work against a joint's normal bending.

Partially because the horse is a quadruped, it has the ability to negotiate very tight circles while remaining relatively perpendicular to the ground. With lateral flexibility in the back and spine enhanced by systematic lateral exercises, and the power to constrict one side of the body while extending the other, the horse is capable of acute lateral circles and turns as long as it keeps its balance upright over its feet.[6]

By comparison, imagine you are riding a bicycle. You need to make a sharp turn so you turn the handlebars and lean into the direction of the turn, tipping the bike on to its side. All of a sudden you realise that the ground is loose gravel, the tyres begin to slip. In a flash you have fallen straight down on your inside shoulder. Anyone who has ever seen a bicycle race in one of the great velodromes with their highly banked walls, realises the limitations of turning a one-tracked creature.

Poor riders can have a similar kind of effect on the horse, nullifying the horse's lateral agility. The mounted rider sits above the horse's natural centre of balance. If the horse is already negotiating a tight curve and the rider leans further into the curve, it can upset the horse's lateral balance drastically. The horse becomes insecure in its vulnerable unbalanced position, and will often take strong rapid, scrambling steps in an effort to re-centre itself and the 'out of sync' rider over its feet. The best riders are keenly aware of the horse's lateral field of balance and over a period of time become so attuned that not only are they not a hindrance to the horse but also in some cases they help maintain even better balancing by acting very subtly as a counter-weight in the most difficult turns.

Through the practice of turns, changes of rein, and especially the lateral exercises, the rider must learn to feel and then to be able to become one with the horse. He must enhance instead of impede its lateral balance.

[6] For background information see, 'Kinematics of the Equine Thoracolumbar Spine,' H. G. G Townsend, D. H. Leach, P. B. Fretz, *Equine Vet. Journal*, 1983, 15(2), pp. 117–122.

Ultimately the pair will be able to perform a movement like a canter pirouette, wherein the horse canters into, around, and then out of the smallest of circles without any loss of the canter rhythm, without leaning or falling over, and without pivoting off frozen hind legs, proving that horse and rider have mastered the lateral field of balance, and not a turning trick.

As I continued riding, the efficiency of my legs depended greatly on the security and balance of my seat. Only when I could sit in balance without holding or gripping with my legs, did my legs then become free to signal and feel the horse. Once they became free, I had to consciously develop their dexterity, especially on my left side which was my stiffer side. The added difficulty was that more often than not, I would be matched to the horse with my weaker, less flexible leg on the stiffer side of the horse, and my more agile leg on the more flexible side of the horse. There was a tendency often to ride unconsciously towards my strength instead of developing my weaker side into better overall balance. I had to make a strong effort in the beginning to practise all the lateral exercises until both sides felt similar. This usually meant much more practice on the stiffer side.

I believe it is helpful to begin to practise leg yielding and simple lateral exercises even before the seat is fully trained. I think they can accelerate the process of learning balance, because in an effort to move the legs independently, the legs will automatically have to release some of their grip. This will help to loosen tension and settle the seat deeper, sooner.

Once the dexterity of both legs is comparable, the legs must then get practice working together through frequent changes of direction and frequent changes of exercise. Like two hands playing a piano, both legs may act independently but must yield a coherent and complementary musical whole. At that point the rider can lose consciousness of the instrument, in this case, the legs, and be aware of the action they can produce – the immediate music. Something mysterious will happen to the western concept of time as one's awareness settles solely into the present action. The rider will be absolutely free. Free of any cumbersome past and devoid of future expectations. It is like stopping time, and the effect is just as rejuvenating.

Chapter Four

So Many Masters

BEFORE I MET MY first wife she had travelled to Ireland
to study with Ian Dudgeon at his riding school. She
talked with admiration about a horsewoman she had
met named Sylvia Stanier. Later it was to happen that I

would see Miss Stanier's writings and use her fine treatise on lungeing. I remembered reading in one of her introductions a thank you to Mr Oliveira. Over a number of years I kept finding or hearing references to Nuno Oliveira, and always from horsemen and -women who themselves were outstanding. I wanted very much to have the chance to experience some other schools of classical horsemanship, and to broaden my education beyond the German tradition I had been following. So when the chance came for me to go to Portugal to watch and work with Nuno Oliveira, I took it.

It is winter and it is dark. I am sitting in the dining room of a small hotel in a little town in Portugal. I am the only guest. There are at least thirty place settings. All the bowls, plates and cups are turned over so that they won't collect dust. Only mine are upright. The woman who runs the place gestures to me to come to the kitchen to see if I like what she is cooking tonight. We have to pass down a narrow corridor. On one side of the corridor is a row of opaque windows. I can make out the shapes of leaves from plants pressed up against the glass. One of the windows has a pane of glass missing at the bottom. As I pass it, the woman's watchdog rams his snapping, growling head through the frame. Finally in the kitchen, I agree to whatever she is cooking. On my way back to the table, I stay close to the wall, but in a second the dog's head shoots through with renewed fury.

Ever since I arrived a few days earlier, I have had a terrible cough. The weather is not extremely cold, although it is frosty at night; but it is very damp. The hotel has no visible means of heating. There is no heat at all in my room. In the room there is a bed and a chair. On the wall there is a calendar from some year gone by. On the chair, as part of the decor, is a large doll. It is the kind of doll that has its eyelids on rollers so they can move up or down. After a while I have to move it. I cannot stand the constant staring, day and night. It becomes eerie. I am always waiting for it to blink.

My cough seems to be getting worse. I sleep in my clothes but still I can't get warm. Everything is wet. My only relief from the night's coughing and freezing spells is some heavy port wine the woman stocks in the dining room. In the middle of the night I think about dying in a place like this and decide I don't want to get much sicker.

After a week, I feel I have to find another place. I cannot get the taxis to drive me over the rough dirt roads to and from the school. I decide to seek new lodgings.

There is a very small village nearer to the school. It has a few houses, and a public well on the main road where herds of goats come to be watered. It feels very isolated. A young woman has some rooms for rent. She is pleasant and when I see there is a portable heater in my room, I am sold.

Each day, as I walk from the village towards the school, the opera music that fills the riding hall can be heard long before I can see the school. Every day I arrive early to watch the youngest horses in training. Later there is the morning lesson and then lunch. After lunch there will be more training until the later afternoon lesson. After the final lesson the students are usually all invited to the small cottage near the riding school. In its library-like office, everyone is offered some port and the day's work may be reviewed, theory discussed, or the Master will simply recount some fascinating story about horses. Afterwards I walk home under the night sky, and then read and study Baucher and Beaudant.

I have been very lucky. Since I arrived here, there has been only one other student, a man from Paris. Thus we get full attention in the lessons. Even though there are very few words of correction, the horses begin training you instantly. You are allowed to try, and to make mistakes. Each day you are asked to do grand prix movements, over and over. First the horses do them for the voice of the Master. Later you follow more closely and become bold enough to ask for them yourself – always quietly, never with the physical straining that you can see in other schools of riding.

As I become immersed in observing and riding these horses, my scepticism changes to wonder. Some beautiful work is being carried out in an entirely different manner. When I say different I mean different, not only in terms of style but also in the actual structure of the training. Horses barely broken to saddle are being taught the ultimate movements of piaffe and passage and flying changes. This is almost the exact opposite of what I am used to, and yet it works.

As I continue to ride and watch these horses daily and compare the training of the young Portuguese horses to the training in the Austro-Hungarian, or the best German schools, an old, moth-eaten debate surfaces. As if some rag or garment lifts itself up and begins to move on its own, I am forced to reconcile the impossible. It is not pages of a book discussing some esoteric semantics that I am facing, but a living, breathing problem. How will I accommodate the two schools of thought concerning 'riding in lightness' on a slack rein, and 'riding in lightness' on a taut, elastic rein?

There is at least one key elemental difference in the training of the youngest dressage horses in the

Portuguese school and those of the Austro-Hungarian or better German schools which are quite similar. The youngest horses in Portugal are very quickly fitted with a full bridle and then ridden on a semi-slack or loose rein. The youngest horses of more central Europe are never fitted early with a full bridle and are always ridden in a snaffle with taut reins. This simple point regarding equipment exposes an underlying paradox. However, the imagined paradoxes may not be paradoxes after all.

When the young horse is fitted with a full bridle, it is reluctant to lean into it. The danger here is that the youngster may fear the bit and stay behind it. But the problem with being behind the bit is not only the visual picture that we see, where the horse's nose is pointed towards its chest and its face is behind the perpendicular line drawn to the ground – this is just an outward manifestation. The important issue or danger is that the horse loses the connection from the rider's hand and leg to the bit and thence to its legs. The rein aid does not go all the way through the horse's back, so there is a gap between the driving power and regulating it. To use a bad analogy it might be like driving a car with a bad clutch. The accelerator roars, but when the clutch is let out to move the car forward, it just slips; it won't catch and move off. Finally it slides less and less and the car moves. Likewise, to stop, the clutch is depressed to relieve the forward drive, but the car keeps going forward. The brakes have to be used to choke off the forward driving power. The car is dangerously late in all its responses because this gap has developed. In the horse that is behind the bit, the head carriage will be false, and the back of the horse will be hollow with the hind legs out behind the horse's balance, not underneath it for immediate response. An easy test to feel if a horse is behind the bit is to send it forward in an extension.

If the steps do not immediately elongate, if the horse does not stretch through the back, then the horse is categorically disconnected and is behind. It is afraid to move through the bridle and is not round.

A very serious mistake of observation can be to assume that because the reins are semi-slack the horse is not up into the bridle. Unless one has truly felt horses that are behind, you can make this mistake quite easily. Instead of 'seeing' (that is, perceiving) the whole horse in its totality – the back, the transitions, the engagement – the novice may just 'look' at the reins. One has to pay attention to the horse's back and the illusive quality of roundness. True exponents of the Portuguese style, riding with 'lightness', are always checking their young horses to see that they come energetically forward from the rider's legs, and they are not leaning on the bridle but will hold themselves in balance. This riding style is particularly harmonious with the types of horses ridden there because they are muscular, with a higher action and a predilection towards early collection. The modern mastery of these riders is clearly proven when these horses are seen to extend their movements with true forward stretching, something they rarely practised in baroque riding. When a dressage horse is ridden through transitions of longitudinal balance – extension and collection – on the lightest of rein aids, it expresses the highest kind of dressage.

When a horse is trained in the snaffle in the manner of the Austro-Hungarian school or the better German schools, the trainers are so concerned with forward riding that some concessions are made in the beginning in terms of sacrificing lightness. Here the young horse is asked to drive off each hind leg powerfully and return it way under its body, to swing freely and engage well. A wave of energy is thrust right up the horse's spine towards the head, lifting the horse's centre of mass and lightening the forehand. The horse's whole back swings and the shoulder reaches out. The correct appearance is one of a well-timed, not fast, full swinging gait with good use of the legs, and with the horse moving through the bridle.

Any hollowness in the horse's back will slice this power wave in two. The horse will be disconnected from front to rear. These trainers will avoid hollowness at all costs, hence the mild snaffle and even some indulgent leaning by the young horse. These horses are taught to feel that they can always move forward. They learn never to fear engaged movement. In this school of riding, collection will develop from gradually mastering control over the forward impulse, training carrying power into the step. If the horse is used to stepping way under the body with free, swinging steps it seems logical that it shouldn't be too difficult to move its centre of balance backwards over these engaged legs and thus free the front end.

However, there is a large danger in this method of training. If a horse is allowed to lean on a mild snaffle or stretch into it while driving forward for too long, it can induce too much thrusting power and no carrying power. The horse can grow quickly accustomed to travelling unbalanced, too far out on the forehand. The back of the horse will become stiff and long, and when it comes to the time to collect the horse, it will be inflexible and unable to shorten its body longitudinally. The rider will have to pull harshly on the reins to get the horse to tip its centre of balance more towards the rear. The irony is that the rider, in an effort to avoid the disuniting factor caused by hollowness, creates a different paralysing stiffness in the back that is equally troublesome.

[71]

The mistake of observation here is to think that the mild bit is equal to mild riding or lightness in the hand. It may very well be that the horse is pulling much harder and causing much more damage to its mouth in the incorrectly used snaffle than it would in a more severe bit, or a correctly used full bridle.

To make the patent statement that the full bridle is more severe than the snaffle seems myopic. Do I mean it is more severe just hanging on the wall? Obviously I am talking about in the horse's mouth and connected to a rider's hand. That is where the trouble begins, because the next question must be, in whose hands?

The best riders of the snaffle school of training never seem to equate 'long and low' with long and heavy. These riders are aware, from the earliest training, of the tempo and balance of their horses. Stretching does not always mean leaning. By using frequent changes of tempo and transitions, these riders are constantly teaching and testing the young horse to seek its own balance. Very often these riders will drop the reins on the leaning horse. In this initial gap the horse lurches forward, as if a crutch on which it had been leaning were kicked out from under its bearing. Soon, however, these horses begin to try to hold themselves up instead of relying on this unreliable support, the smart rider's hands.

In an effort to seek some reconciliation in the old semantics, I am in a funny place. The closer one gets to the world of action, the fewer differences there seem to be among the best riders. Riding in lightness seems to be more universal and more true. In my mind's eye I liken it to a map with a circular road on it. There is no point in rushing to the end, because it is only the beginning where you have already been. If you ride lightly enough, you may come free from apparent diversions, inevitable destinations. Regardless, it is the riding, not the road.

Perhaps there is an element of pragmatism in the choice of these bits. In the rounder breeds, like the Andalusians, Lusitanos and Lipizzaners, there is less worry about hollowness. Therefore, the full bridle is less ominous. The longer, flatter horses of more central Europe have greater facility in the extended paces. With their great reach they are more susceptible to hollowness in the back, hence perhaps the popularity of the snaffle. Whatever the historical reasons for this equipment it seems clearer to me that it has little to do with 'riding in lightness'.

A month has passed by. The school is still not busy. A few different Europeans have come in for a couple of days, and have left.

This weekend two women from Belgium are here, and on this day a well-known trainer from France's elite cavalry school, the Cadre Noir, is here to ride some horses and visit the Master. He watches the lessons and some of the practice with as much intent as anyone else. This evening we are all going out to dinner as guests of the Master. This will be only the second time in a month that I have been out of the tiny village.

It is raining. We all drive in different cars. I go with the Master and his wife; his son drives. I do not think Mr Oliveira even has a driver's licence and as far as I can tell he has no interest in mechanical things, other than his stereo which brings him, above all, his beloved music of Verdi. We are driving in the dark. I have no idea where we are going. It seems we must be getting nearer to the ocean. I swear I can feel the air off the sea. When we arrive we are the only people in the restaurant. There are familiar seafood decorations and

[73]

the fish looks like it will be good. The meals come slowly. Much of the table conversation is in French although the Master makes several interruptions with political questions in English about the United States. Before much longer, the conversation is thickly into horses. The Belgian woman next to me tries to translate as much as she can. Finally the subject of the Spanish Riding School comes up, and there is criticism of its current work. It is not malicious, though perhaps some is motivated by nationalism. Some of the objections are very technical, like the angulation of the half pass; some are more encompassing, like objections about lightness. The feel of this discussion is so familiar to me it begins to set up an eerie kind of *déjà vu*. The resonances of the language have the same physical sensations as a kind of motion sickness. It is literally making me feel ill. My head is turning my stomach. There is an antagonism inside me stirring around. I finish the meal, but I feel cold. Something continues to irritate me. I would prefer to go out, to be alone. The rest of the evening is pure discipline. I wait it out. When I am finally back in my room, I think about it all night.

The next day is Sunday. There is no riding at the school. I hitchhike a ride to the coast, to a small fishing village and resort. The shops are all closed, but I feel better just wandering through the streets. I am still unnerved by the conversation the night before. If I were at the Spanish Riding School, I wonder, would I hear similar criticisms of other schools? What is it about these obvious and even understandable loyalties that keeps turning and folding my stomach over, again and again? There is something else going on. I follow one of the narrow, steep streets to the floor of the harbour. All the dories are docked on the shore. A couple of fishermen are there, but although they are tending the boats they are not dressed for work. From this harbour I see an old white hotel that sits on a point that juts out into the ocean. At the end of the point the high surf is breaking over the rock. White surf slides in all directions, cleaning the smooth grey stone. I decide to see if I can get closer to that closed-down hotel. After a twenty-minute walk I am on the street that goes down to the hotel. Off to the left I see a beautiful sandy beach, backed by a wall of rock that rises straight up at least one hundred feet. I find my way down to the beach. It is deserted. There is too much cold spray. I am getting wet and cold. I look up to the top of the cliffs. I can see a road and some houses off behind it. I think it will be nicer up there. After a climb, I sit down on the sandy grass and, in the full sun of the afternoon, look out over the Atlantic. To the right the surf curls up on to the point where the hotel is. I am certain that in a storm the water must reach right into the building. It must be incredible. I wonder if it is ever open?

Below me the beach fills the quarter mile or so of the cove; beyond that I can see miles of the coast of Portugal. Even way up here I can feel damp spray from time to time as it is lifted up the face of rock by the wind and the heat. I look out over the ocean. The waves roll steadily. I think of the potential of each wave. I see it travelling right across the Atlantic to the east coast of America. In my mind I see the eastern shore of the United States. Soon the problem retakes the forefront of my attention. I keep asking myself, over and over, how can all these masters be wrong? Who is doing it right? The afternoon passes. I wonder where I will have to go next to see and learn to do it right? The question seems to tie itself to the rhythm of the waves. The noise of the sea muffles other sounds. I feel my own voice come up again. It is pushing me, prodding me every time I seem to get sleepy. I begin to get the feeling that if I look hard enough I will be able to see America. I feel a pull by the waves both in my stomach and in my concentration. Something is trying to break out. I run through all the teachers I have known, the statements of many, the different schools of thought. Each master appears before me in a stylised portrait. How can they all be wrong?

Then, almost at dusk, in all its ridiculous simplicity, I feel the answer. All the tension is gone. Nothing obstructs me from America. In one step I have returned home for a moment. These masters are not all wrong. They are all right! There are great piaffes in Portugal, but there are great piaffes in France, Russia, England, Spain, Austria and Germany; and there are great piaffes in America. How could five, ten or fifteen horses be trained differently and independently, yet all be doing the exact same movement correctly? It is now clear to me that different paths can lead to the same result. In western education we are so steeped in our precious scientific method that it seems inconceivable that there could be more than one correct answer for a question or problem. In reality there are all kinds of correct answers simultaneously existing side by side. You can take your pick. They will all work if correctly applied. There seems to be no such thing as only one correct answer, but there is only one correct way of answering.

I feel an instantaneous and tremendous relief. I understand the source of the antagonism during the dinner conversation. My own choice of loyalties seems liberated. It is simple. I don't have to choose. I can accommodate them all. There is infinite room. I realise a very important phase of my apprenticeship is complete. It is time now for me to try my own way. There will be room for this American's way as well. I will have to do it myself. I have to find my own path in order to have any chance at completing my training. I look out across the ocean. It is almost dark. I know what I have to do. Within one week I am flying back to the United States by way of Montreal, Canada.

While the quiet plane is streaking through the dark, my mind is filled with images of Oliveira, and his complete mastery. I am in awe of his artistry and skill, his control on the lightest of aids. One particular incident comes to mind.

At one end of his indoor school is an observation room. It has windows along its entire length so quite a few people can observe at once. From the windows there is roughly an eight-feet drop to the riding-hall floor. On this particular day the weather was terrible, and it happened that I was the only person in the observation room and Nuno was the only person riding. He was working a young grey stallion through some lateral work at the trot, and in the last few days he had been teaching this young horse the flying changes during the canter work. Very quickly the sky became dark. His methodic work continued quietly. The air became so still that it was easy to hear the horse chewing the bit even when it was at the farthest end of the school. Suddenly, in one flash a storm erupted. Lightning crackled and sheets of hail-like rain pounded the thin metal roof of the arena. The grey horse exploded and began blazing around the arena in half spins and huge leaps. As they passed in front of me, the horse caprioled right up alongside the windows. Oliveira was inches from me, flying through the air. The thunder crashed and the roof sounded as though it would collapse at any moment. The horse became even more frenzied, and went tearing around the hall again. Mr Oliveira's face was turning deeper and deeper shades of red. I was certain that in another second he was going to be thrown, and thrown hard. Oddly enough, what was going through my mind was what I should do if that happened. There is no entrance directly from the observation room to the school. You have to go out the back, down a flight of stairs outside, then enter the school by a side door. It would take for ever to get to him and his horse. I thought about jumping from the windows. It wouldn't have been a big jump; however, this place was like a church and I wasn't sure what would happen to me, no matter what the reason, after such a breach of protocol. I was half standing when the horse and Oliveira went by again, as much in the air as on the ground. Amazingly, throughout this performance his position hardly moved. He sat bolt upright. Only his extremely flushed face and his surprised eyes revealed his effort to stay on board. Finally, after what seemed like at least three or four full minutes, he settled the horse down. The storm eased and my own pulse began to recover. When Oliveira worked he hardly ever looked up to the observation room. But this time after he had the horse calmly walking, he glanced up towards me and smiled. I thought that deep inside it had been fun for him. I couldn't wait until the evening after work when I could go to his little office for some port and conversation with him. As the day went on and I thought about it, I was more and more impressed by the fact that he never admonished the horse but only comforted him.

Later that evening a couple of people showed up at his office. The small room was filled with books and photographs of some of his horses. A small kerosene heater glowed red as it wicked off the dampness. As he came in I was first to go to him. I told him I thought that that was some ride today. This time he laughed. I asked him very honestly if he had always had the amount of patience that he seemed to have so much of now. He looked at me squarely, and said, 'Of course not.' He told me he had done all kinds of crazy things when he was young, but that he had been riding for a very long time, and that it gets better. It was clear to me that he was emphasising the practice and not to worry. That it would come along by itself.

Now on the plane I think about patience and wonder if it isn't the greatest gift a horseman can receive. When I see the mountains of Canada, I feel very strong. I am only miles from my old Adirondack farm when we rest at the airport. I feel good, and yet I am apprehensive as to what will happen next.

Chapter Five

Technique and Poetry

'I WANT TO MAKE SURE they're not so concerned with technical precision that they'll miss the poetic content of the music. On the other hand they can only illuminate the poetic content when they're able to forget about technique entirely.'

Jorge Mester, on teaching a conducting class at the Juilliard School of Music in New York City.

When a rider/trainer begins to work with horses without the aid of a teacher's guiding eye, the limits of his technique quickly surface. For me it was no different. I constantly questioned my own technique and form. It seemed as if I would have to come to terms with the fact that I might never have the technique I thought I should have. If technique were all that mattered and I might never have enough, I was going to have a hard time not seeing this as a complete failure.

I began to review my feelings about technique. I knew that technique could always be improved: there were small flaws in many of the masters. Yet a perplexing phenomenon was that as many masters became older and lost a certain amount of physical strength, ability, hand–eye coordination, and many of the things normally connected with technique, these masters did not become worse riders and trainers: they usually became better. That fact alone made me suspicious of making technique the end-all. However, in riding the expression of the music in the riding (or the art) is incomprehensible without considerable riding technique.

Imagine a horse and rider cantering on a true canter, that is, cantering on the right lead when going to the right, and/or left lead when going to the left. The difference in leads in a general way corresponds to left-handedness and right-handedness in human beings. Every stride of the canter of a given lead has three beats: a single hind foot strikes the ground as the first beat; a diagonal pair of legs strikes at once for the second beat; and finally the lone remaining foreleg strikes for the third beat. At the end of this sequence there is a moment of suspension, and then the pattern is repeated. In high school work and at upper levels since the time of Baucher, one canter exercise has been to deliberately change from one lead to another during the moment of

[81]

suspension. This amounts to a kind of instantaneous symmetrical change along the axis of the horse's spine. In the highest tests of riding today, not only is it demanded that the rider be able to control the number of these changes, but also the intervals of strides between each change. For example, the horse and rider may execute four complete canter strides on the right, do a flying change in the moment of suspension and continue with four strides on the left, flying change back to the right, etc. This exercise can be increased in difficulty by doing the flying changes after every three strides, or two, and finally after every single stride.

There are two main methods that I use to teach the flying change. Each has its good points and I use whichever one seems to fit the horse better. One way is to circle the horse at canter. As I complete the circle, I make a downward transition to trot. I change the bend to the opposite direction, strike off on the opposite lead and circle in that direction. When I come back to the middle, I go back to trot, change direction and go off again on the opposite lead. As the horse becomes more proficient, I reduce the number of trot strides until, when I feel the horse is ready, I skip the trot entirely, asking with firm aids to change leads from canter to canter, through the flying change. Since this method is carried out in the open, away from any wall for support or guidance, some horses will swing out sideways too much.

Under the other system, I canter down the long side of the ring or arena, and about half way down, I start a small circle. Instead of completing it, half way around I head back to the wall on a small diagonal. When I return to the wall, I will be counter-cantering and about to ride through the corner of the arena. Just as I approach the corner I ask for a change. Often the horse obliges because it prefers to return to the true canter. Also, the relief from the extra stretch of the counter-canter is welcome. This method has the benefit of being next to a wall when changing, which helps to keep the horse straighter.

As soon as I began to teach horses flying changes it became very apparent why it was so necessary to teach the horse straight strike-offs in the beginning, making sure as a rider to use both legs to execute canter departures. I quickly saw how, by using one leg more strongly, be it outside behind the girth or inside on the girth, I could unconsciously develop a slight swing in the horse's body, away from the stronger leg at the moment of the strike-off. In the flying change, and even more so in the multiple flying changes, the horse could sway from side to side, and any time the horse deviates sideways it will automatically be less forward, and obviously less straight.

I am trying to teach an ex-racehorse the flying change. This particular horse is presenting some new problems which I have never faced. He is properly prepared in that he will strike off quietly and accurately on either lead in any direction. His counter-canter is confirmed. Everything is in place.

As I begin the flying changes a pattern quickly develops. Whichever system I try, if I ask too vigorously for the change, the horse leaps up into the air practically in a capriole, my back is wrenched by the great twist and kick, and when we hit the ground we are off and running. When I tone down my aids and ask gently, the horse seems to get lazy and changes first with his front legs and then late with his hind ones. It is very smooth and therefore very hard to feel, but almost always incorrect. There does not seem to be any middle ground.

[83]

At least a month goes by. I am essentially working alone and it is getting frustrating. There doesn't seem to be any progress. The changes are either calm and late, or they are wild. More time passes. I am in one of those training caves and there is no teacher to guide me out. I am stuck. The knowledge I have acquired up until now is not adequate. I have to find something new.

I decide to go to the indoor riding school. It has a large mirror in the middle of the short wall. I ride across the arena. I check my position and go through all the fundamentals. Straight, simple changes. I check myself to see that I am not crooked. I tell myself to stay calm, to give myself a chance to work through it. I try to be aware and feel what is going on. I decide to canter a series of serpentines. My intention is to try to change at every change of rein in the middle. At the time this is no stroke of training genius, but I do have two reasons. The primary one is that I will be able to see the changes in the mirror – if the changes become too smooth for me to feel, maybe I can see something in our reflection. The second reason is that I am hoping to use anticipation in a productive way. If the horse knows the change is coming every time we cross the centre line, maybe he will get a little ahead of me. Even if he changes before I ask, it will be a step in the right direction. There is a risk, however, that the obedience I have in the counter-canter will deteriorate if I do manage to get him changing every time. How am I going to make him hold the counter-canter in future? I decide to deal with that later.

On the first day indoors, we carry out a whole series of changes. When I feel the horse tiring, I quit. None is really correct, but I stay calm. I tell myself to wait. I listen intently. A few days pass. I am getting nervous about doing so many changes incorrectly. I am not sure

how much longer I can be patient before I start trying
something else, but I continue. More time passes. The
changes still have not improved, but some related things
have surprisingly begun to change. I have found that
simply by doing the serpentines and asking for the
changes in the middle of the shorter width of the arena,
the horse is reluctant to take the wild leaps he would
take if we were out in the open. The walls of the arena
seem naturally to contain him. Even if I ask fairly
strongly, the horse immediately faces the opposite wall
of the arena and then a short turn into the next serpentine. Without the wild leap, I am less protective in my
own position. I soften my seat, and sit deeper. The result
is a much better feel. Furthermore with this natural
confinement I find I use much less hand to control the
horse. As soon as I let go with my hands, the gait
becomes freer and the balance shifts more towards the
rear, as I send the horse forward with my seat and legs.
The immediate turns at the wall into the next loop of
each serpentine emphasise the change of bend and this
seems important to this horse. He seems much less
confused when I make sure the bending is consistent
and deliberate in both directions. I cannot be too
straight. The turns have an added benefit of collecting
the horse, thus balancing him more towards the rear.
The more days I spend going through the pattern, the
more I learn about changes. Very soon for the first time,
the percentage of correct changes begins to increase. I
can ride with less hand and the result is more lively
steps; the changes automatically become straighter as
the horse goes more forward and less sideways. With
the balance better shifted off the front, the changes are
much less likely to be late. The more relaxed the horse
is with the habit of the exercise, the easier it is to do
the changes. Soon they are so good that I try some

along the wall, where I can work on straightening them even more. It is clear now that although there is still a lot of polishing to do, the horse understands what I am asking.

My ideas on technique seemed to be settling somewhere in between those who said 'since technique is obviously separate from art, if you are interested in art then forget technique', and those who obsessively drilled their scales and movements of technique for the sake of discipline alone. These great technicians seemed to be crying out in strange ways for some release from their inevitably declining skill.

When I went into that indoor school I had my mental processes backed into a corner. I had no plan. I went inside with the idea of opening up my practice. What I really discovered was not so much how to teach one horse the flying change; instead I learned the power of the double-edged sword of technique. First, in order to 'understand' any problem with a horse, I found I needed good technique to feel what was going on. Then, practically simultaneously, the other edge of technique made me act on what I had perceived to effect the ride. As soon as I saw this, I sensed the urgency of good position. Good form is not some esoteric exercise, some historical theatre. No. It is very, very practical. It is language. If, as a rider, I cannot keep my legs in place and also have good dexterity, it will not matter how much I know about the difficulty – I will never be able to have any effect on it. I would not like to claim that these specific exercises had any magical qualities: my point is almost the opposite. I have begun to see that it is often more important *how* an exercise is done and not what *is* done. In repetitions the troublesome subtleties can surface as the rider feels them over and over. I think it is fair to say that a good teacher could have saved me a lot of time by pinpointing difficulties from the ground, but the interesting thing was that the spirit of the movements was beginning to reveal itself to me up in the saddle and perhaps equally important, I was beginning to be able to influence it. Travel along the road was beginning to go both ways.

When, as a rider and trainer, I rode into the dark recesses of training problems without the guiding torch of a teacher, it was the discipline from my constant practice of technique that kept me from panicking and running in every direction looking for a way out. I simply continued to ride every day, trying to remain as open and calm as possible, and inevitably, although sometimes after a long time, I saw light and a way out was revealed. After each time I grew less afraid of the dark and I let the answers find me. It was the discipline achieved from the practice of technique that eventually could give me some freedom to go into the unknown without the paralysis of fear.

Good technique probably best manifests itself in the rider's form on a horse. Only in the proper form will the rider be able to perceive what is happening as he rides, especially if he rides into problems. Only in good form will the rider be able to effect a correction. Good technique is simultaneously reading the situation and acting on it. In the end, good technique can allow the rider freedom. If the rider never ventures beyond the technique, then the rider, even if a supreme technician, will leave a heavy stamp. Horses trained in this way will not likely step out from under this total and constant manipulation and submission. If the rider uses the technique to help let go, then new original solutions can be found. All the time one can tap the unconscious, and horses will take steps on their own. Their exhibitions become artistic presentations. One has to be warned

[87]

that unless the practice is flowing and not fixated, it can degenerate into a trap where the technician tries to force perfection. If you are only interested in future goals you can defeat yourself, because you stifle your perceptive qualities by ordering their attention instead of letting them soak into everything around you, which is what they do best. The rider's practice must develop his or her awareness of movements, not just the incessant execution of movements.

Knowing that technique could always be improved gave me some relief from my image of perfection, which was some static state that you could only reach by obsessive practice of technique. In my vision of perfection everything was perfectly controlled, and yet this image is almost the exact opposite description of art, which is creative, free, open and almost perfectly uncontrolled. I began to see technique as only a tool, a discipline to help you remain stable when facing the unconscious, the creative, the fear of the unknown, and the new. I found some breathing room to allow myself to experiment, to experience without constant stifling comparison and measurement. I was beginning to gain a certain confidence in my work.

Furthermore, knowing that improving the technique will not necessarily improve the art, made technique seem more humble. I could place technique in a more natural and harmonious perspective. The effect was that it relieved an incredible amount of pressure I had built up on and around perfecting technique.

The beautiful and mysterious reward was that as soon as I took the importance off of technique, it automatically improved immeasurably.

Chapter Six

Prize Riding

'A MAN WHO IS completely absorbed in his technical skill degenerates into a "function", a cog in a machine. One who devotes one's life whole-heartedly to the Way of the Samurai does not become the devotee of a particular skill and does not allow oneself to be treated as a simple function. . . . When a Samurai prepares himself mentally to bear single-handedly the burden of the whole (*han*), when he applies himself to his work with great self-confidence, he ceases to be a mere function. He is a *samurai*. He is the Way of the Samurai. There

[89]

is no fear that such a human being will degenerate into a mere cog in the social machine. However, a man who lives for his technical proficiency cannot fulfil his total human role; all he can do is perform a single function, especially in a technology-oriented society such as ours. If a Samurai who cherishes a total human ideal gives himself over to a particular talent or skill, his whole ideal will be eaten away by his specific function. This is what Jocho (author of *Hagakure*) fears. His image of the ideal human being is not a compromise product: one part function to one part total being. A total person does not need a skill. He represents spirit, he represents action, he represents the ideal principles on which his realm is founded.'

Yukio Mishima[1]

What is Mishima's statement about? What could it possibly have to do with riding? In Jocho Yamamoto's book, *Hagakure*,[2] there is an expressed contempt for technical precision, yet in the techniques of Japanese tea ceremonies, and in Japanese *Haiku* poetry, there seems almost fanatic attention to technique. So how does the total person, the true person, pay attention to technique and not pay attention to technique?

I believe looking at the relationship between classical dressage riding and current prize dressage riding can illuminate this apparent paradox, and show how current the fears of Yamamoto and Mishima still are.

Classical dressage riding is quite old. The writings of Xenophon, a student of Socrates, are still admired today for their humane and gentle approach to horsemanship. Representations of dressage movements practised today

[1] MISHIMA, YUKIO, *The Way of the Samurai*, Peregree Books, 1977.
[2] YAMAMOTO, JOCHO AND TASHIRO, TSURAMOTO, *Hagakure*, 1659–1719.

are visible in Greek art that is over two thousand years old. Prize riding, that is the riding of predetermined tests in a competition against other riders and horses, is relatively new.

As an art form, classical dressage riding has a strong similarity to certain kinds of rigidly stylised Japanese arts – *Haiku* (poetry) and painting, for example. In these arts we see that the artist is subject to some relatively strict rules of structure in which he must work. In Japanese *Haiku* poems, the structure is quite defined. The poems are always in three lines and contain seventeen syllables. In classical dressage there are only a relatively small number of movements to be performed at the high school. No matter where you travel – France, England, Germany, Austria, Russia, Denmark, America, Mexico – you will recognise the piaffe, the passage, canter pirouettes, etc., and artists who choose to work in these forms accept the stiff structure and focus their creativity on the execution within these structures.

The *Haiku* poet focuses his attention on new and personal ways to express something within this style. As impossible as it sounds, no two poems are alike, and furthermore, there seems to be no end to the supply of these original works. They are as infinite as creation itself.

In classical dressage the movements performed are representations of natural movements that a horse might do at play or in courtship or territorial displays. This has been *the* central element in describing the classical riding approach – that is, that the movements must complement nature, and what is natural for the horse.

Historically fantastic gaits or gimmicks of movement fall into the category of circus. It is in the circus, after all, where, by its own definition, the unusual and fantastic are displayed. In the circus or in circus riding the

[91]

emphasis is always on the trick and less on the process. The end result must be obvious, dramatic, thrilling and, above all, entertaining for the large audiences who come to have fun and generally cannot sit too close to the performers. The circus is not the place for subtleties.

Throughout the history of riding there have been bitter and inconclusive arguments as to which movements are really natural to the horse. Alois Podhajsky[3], the late director of the Spanish Riding School, has written that such debates went on inside the citadel of classical equitation, the great Spanish Riding School, itself. Flying changes at every stride, for example, have been such a debatable movement. Flying changes at every stride, in fact even single flying changes, were not practised (as far as I have been able to determine) in the baroque days of la Guerinière. The invention or creation of this movement is generally credited to François Baucher, a controversial, spectacular rider who performed with the circus of Laurent and Adolphe Franconi. Podhajsky once stated that the question of flying changes at every stride had never been resolved in Vienna, yet today they are accepted and are universally performed and exhibited even at that same school.

Much of the time it is not the movement in itself which determines the kind of riding, but the whole approach or philosophy of the training. It is often much easier to see the differences if one looks at the more acceptable, conventional, even simpler exercises, instead of the controversial ones. Holes in the fundamentals will show up readily in the most basic patterns and changes of gait or tempo.

The riders' and trainers' tasks are to execute, within strict structures, something that is unique to the spirit

[3] PODHAJSKY, ALOIS, *The Complete Training of the Horse and Rider in the Principles of Classic Horsemanship*, Wiltshire Book Co., 1967.

of a particular horse. One thousand horses may stand side by side in the piaffe and no two will be the same. The rider and horse's range of expression, like the poems, is also as infinite as creativity itself.

Something very interesting happened in poetry over the years since *Haiku* in Japan and rhyming verse in the West became popular, perhaps because a new generation had a need to experiment, to rebel from the ways of the previous generation. Perhaps it was no more than a very physical and natural cycle, like the rise and fall of a wave, in this case the waves of change. Nevertheless some of the newer poets could not see any reason to have their art and their freedom restricted by these strict structures of form. The newer poetry began to experiment with the structure itself. New poets, like the new painters, focused their creative powers less on the object to be explored within the old strict structure, and more on the structure itself. When ten painters stood side by side and painted a red apple, some apples came out square, some were a different colour, some were unrecognisable as apples. This creation was naturally shocking. The artists seemed to be inventing a new language that only they understood. Were they mad? Was there some conscious attempt to exclude viewers and readers? Was the work too personal, and too far beyond any attempt at communication? Far beyond any art that had preceded it?

The best of this kind of art had just as much integrity as the best rhymed verse, or the best *Haiku*. The artists went deep inside themselves, deep inside the world that was presented to them to find their own world. They tried to feel and see, and go as close to the real source of creativity as possible. Their real struggle was to be free. This could certainly include being free of any precedent around them. If they could be free, they could find originality itself. If it is possible for an artist to push away all contrived goals, pre-suppositions, then they can arrive also at their true selves. Originality, creativity, is also truth. The art becomes very naturally self-enlightening, at the very least. It is self-transforming.

Almost all art forms have followed similar transform-ations – similar shifts of creative focus, from execution within the bounds of strict structure, to creating with the structure itself. The worst of this art is so disem-bodied that it is psychotic – by which I mean that no matter how revolutionary one tries to be, there are always some boundaries, some limitations in terms of health or sanity. Suppose a choreographer of ballet had a dream in which dancers standing on two feet rotated their upper bodies through 360° without moving their feet. Well, the human body cannot twist completely around in a circle without breaking. Suppose this chore-ographer pursued this dream anyway and began forcing his dancers to stretch and stretch – ignoring nature's laws. This work then becomes psychotic. It is damaging, impossible and against life. It is unintelligible and self-defeating. Poetry can be psychotic – and certainly some horse training can definitely be psychotic.

Interestingly enough, many modern poets who are comfortable in a wilder, free-flowing style, have had an interest from time to time in working in *Haiku*. When they do, they accept the structure and create within it. There is nothing impossible about making the shift.

To me this is the site where a lot of the confusion between classical dressage and prize riding starts. Classi-cal dressage riding is a living *art* form, and the prac-titioner must adhere to its structure. If you want to invent new movements to experiment with the structure, you can, but you move away from the realm of classical dressage. In classical dressage the creative focus is in exploring the personality of a particular horse's movement, within the structure of the art. Whilst all piaffes, for example, are recognisable as piaffes, the true classicist's creative attention will be to find the purest piaffe for that particular horse; a piaffe, recognisable as piaffe, but unlike any other horse's piaffe; this individual horse's ultimate piaffe. The piaffe itself is not as important as *how* the horse piaffes. This horse's best piaffe is a proof of true training. Ultimately there is a similarity of art because the true artist is not burdened by the structure of the piaffe – any more than the true poet is burdened by the structure of *Haiku*. This is precisely how, referring to the beginning of this chapter, a total and true person can pay attention to technique and not pay attention to technique. In the same way, the true artistic rider knows there is a movement called piaffe – but how his horse does it is where art comes in. There is no ultimate piaffe, any more than there is an ultimate poem. There is only the ultimate piaffe for a particular horse, just like there can only be an ultimate poem for a particular poet. The true piaffe, the true work of art, is by definition original.

This is where prize riding comes into some serious problems relating to the art of dressage. Even though prize riding today consists of relatively the same movements as classical dressage, there is a problem.

We know that if we assemble any fifteen horses, we will have fifteen different piaffes. Now, however, for the sake of scoring, a judge must decide which piaffe is best. Subjection enters the picture, and there is quantification and qualification of art. This is impossible. We know from history what a poor record critics, judges, and societies at large have at recognising great art when it is under their nose. The artist whose work was ignored until after his death was not the exception. That artist was the rule. Few societies are comfortable with the artist whose chief concern is a freedom from precedents and restraint. Too much freedom can lead to social anarchy. Too much originality makes it difficult to move society *en masse*. So it is logical, if nothing else, that a society moves slowly in recognising its misfits. We also know that art is as personal and individual as each artist's fingerprint, or each horse's whorl patterns. There can be so much difference that there won't even be any points of comparison.

However, if contests are to occur, then subjective idealised movements have to be in the mind's eye of the judge in order to render comparison. One piaffe might be deemed better than another because it is closer to the piaffe which the judge believes to be the correct piaffe. The experienced prize rider is aware of this process. The technician knows this; he knows what forms are most acceptable, or popular. He or she chooses and trains horses that best display these forms. He or she practises these forms. The trouble is that the movements become disembodied from the art. They become an end in themselves. This unconnectedness is the opposite of true dressage. This is also the opposite of true art, for now the movements are no longer original. They are contrived, very conscious, imitative.

Imagine a prize *Haikuist*, who realises that *Haikus* about flowers are winning acclaim, recognition, fame and prizes at *Haiku* competitions. This *Haiku* writer begins writing *Haikus* about flowers. As soon as a conscious decision is made to control the creative process, it automatically loses its originality, its freedom. It is reasoned and trapped. This artist has cut off the path that leads to new territory.

Back to the apparent paradox between Mishima's

words and the Japanese culture. The strict structure of *Haiku* challenges the true artist to go beyond it. Faking an artistic attempt – be it a contrived *Haiku* or a contrived piaffe that the current judges hold in high regard – does not work; not because you can't fool others, but because you can't fool yourself. True art always has this integrity, beyond the technical skill. It has the power to transform the self, to enlighten the self, stemming from control of the self. The true artist, then, is the true man or true woman. Their art is not something high and mighty, esoteric and lofty, with its intention on what people think when looking at it. It is a very practical art. The true art becomes not the art of painting, writing, or riding, but of living, living your own life.

Jocho's disdain for the technician is a disdain for someone who plays a game separate from life; one who consciously aims at targets, one who bases his performance on external messages, or ideas. This is a man or woman who has given up him- or herself, and the very thing that makes him or her unique and original, to an idea of how their life should be or how they wish it to be, or how others think it should be. Such a life becomes a ship without its own integral source of power or guidance. It will move wherever it is pushed, even if it means its own demise. Here is the clue as to how an individual loses his freedom.

When a rider begins to ride for conceptions, ideas of what riding is, and not for the true real action of riding itself, he can enter an imaginary world of intellection which has very little to do with a real world. Invariably the body realises this and the disharmony between mind and body – intellection and action – can be devastating to a personality.

Riding to win, or for high scores, or for the opinion of others, leads one into a strange world of external pressures that can destroy riders and horses. When the rider/artist gives up control, he gives up his only real chance to be free. I believe that all these riders are innately aware of their deal with the devil. I also believe that subconsciously they feel imprisoned and this negative feeling eventually swallows up the love and freedom that attracted them to riding in the first place.

I remember a brief conversation I once had with a man who judged riding competitions. In just a few short sentences the man unwittingly revealed much about himself and his life. This judge was noted for being particularly vitriolic in his criticism and scoring of rides. He was middle-aged and at a time in his life when dressage riders are often reaching a peak, but he was not riding. It came out during a serious conversation that he did not ride because he said he could not do it perfectly and therefore he chose not to do it at all. My first instinct was to dismiss this as talk. However, some years went by and I saw he was sticking to his words. He was judging more and more often and still not riding. In this unfolding live theatre, I began to get a sense of the magnitude of the tragedy and especially how serious were Mishima's and Jocho's warnings about losing one's self. Over a period of time, this apparently intelligent man had created a conception about what riding should be. His conception of ideal riding became more and more formidable over the years, until he felt he could not measure up to it. He had created for himself a demon and then he consciously let the demon devour him.

It was apparent that he had a love for riding. What else could have sustained his interest for so long? Even now, defeated by his own creation, he still judged every weekend just to be around riding. No wonder his critiques were vitriolic. Who knows what bitterness he kept within for the thing that tore him away from his beloved riding?

To all outward appearances, this man was highly disciplined but inside he lacked the self-control and strength to resist the challenges of external pressures. To resist the life of the technician as opposed to the life of the artist, or the true man or woman, he sadly let conceptions grow so unchecked by action and reality that his own ideas became too powerful. He intimidated himself, and in the process destroyed his real love in life. The mind can not only freeze the body in terms of immediate reflexes and responses but it also has the power to create permanent paralytic effects as well, as in this case.

It is a hot day. If too many horses are working at once dust drifts upwards like smoke filtering the bright sun. I am judging some dressage classes at a special horse show for handicapped riders. Apart from my secretary, I am alone. We are sited away from the main show traffic, and it is quiet and peaceful. For some years before this, I have been teaching a few instructors of handicapped riders. One year they asked me to judge the dressage at their annual show. I told them that I didn't really judge, but nevertheless they wanted me to do it. I was confronted by blind and deaf riders; children with cerebral palsy, muscular dystrophy, Down's syndrome, brain damage and spina bifida. I felt I needed to be a physician to even begin to give some kind of appraisal of their performances. However, I was so inspired by the courage of these riders that when asked again to judge, I always accepted and even agreed to do other larger shows.

The show that I am at this day is a big show. There are disabled riders from all over. The atmosphere is festive. The range of disabilities is complete. When I first arrive at a show like this I am always a little uneasy. There are so many sad cases – some very severe, and often young children. I don't see many handicapped people from day to day, and the emotional pull can be strong. However, the people are all so friendly and the atmosphere is alive and casual. I get used to it very quickly. I always marvel at the total absence of any kind of prejudice by the horses. They are fine examples. We seem to have lost a lot of natural qualities as we have become so apparently intelligent.

Every time I judge at these shows I experience a familiar feeling. It is the same feeling I get when I am around an outstanding teacher. I see qualities I wish I could develop in myself. I see a certain integrity or a fairness; in other cases a simple fearlessness to try something new; or a ferocity of life, often a plain reluctance to presume something about someone else. Maybe my reasons for coming are selfish, because I always walk away so inspired, flushed with possibilities and charged with energy.

A young girl rides into the arena. The test consists of simple walk and trot manoeuvres. She has very spasmodic hands. It seems difficult for her even to hold the reins. She salutes me before beginning the main body of the test. For me, it is more like the bowing in martial arts, a gesture of mutual respect. She begins the patterns. The horse, like all these horses, is patient and carefully trained. I have seen these horses being groomed in barns by children in wheelchairs. They can be bumped about and vaulted on and off. They seem to revel in the attention. This girl struggles in the first turns. Her hands are almost erupting, but she finishes the circle. She reverses the direction to begin symmetrical patterns. As she turns I notice her eyes. I thought I knew something about controlling uncontrollable hands; I thought I knew something about holding down a wild body – certainly I have been struggling with the elusive roundness of a simple circle for a decade. But when I see the mastery in her young eyes, I don't think I have scratched the surface. I am struck with a wave of ambivalence about being anyone's judge.

After her ride in comes a beautiful Asian child with Down's syndrome. His thick-set pony walks in like some great sage returning from his mountainous retreat. He walks humbly but cannot hide the light of all his wisdom. It seems proper that only an innocent child could be a true friend of a creature of such wisdom.

Before a break, a young woman rides in. The tempo is quicker and the test is more difficult. Her face shows strain. I cannot tell if it is the heat or her concentration. I am aware of the difficulty, but she almost has it hidden. I am impressed by her test. It is very well done. At the final salute, she looks tired. Her face has lost colour. I think it is a very good ride. I am mentally scoring it and composing my remarks as she rides towards the exit. Just out of the gate she slumps and begins to fall from her horse. The ever-attentive aides catch her. They attend to her quickly. I stand up. My pulse quickens. I step out into the arena. She regains consciousness whilst being helped off the horse. Her helpers tell me she has fainted from exhaustion, and that she will recover. As I stand there in the empty dressage ring it hits me that what I have just witnessed is what Zen masters have written about for centuries: a way to live your life so completely that in each experience you hold nothing back; you do something fearlessly, live every moment as if it were your last, then life takes on the importance it was meant to have. Just a few moments ago, in front of me, I saw this perfection of action, so perfectly timed that for the rider there was nothing left.

Inside I begin to swell. What am I doing here judging? Who do I think I am, assigning my stupid little numbers to a perfect performance – one that embodies all that a person can possibly give. I am inwardly furious with myself. I try to blame the organisers. Why is it that every time four Americans get together and do the same activity, they find a way to make rules so they can rank each other?

I am glad there is a break. I try to calm down, and go off to find something to eat. I walk around the show trying to make some sense of my dilemma. I watch some other classes. I listen to the competitors, and instructors. I wish I could talk to some more experienced teachers. Maybe they could give me some perspective, but they are obviously all busy. I keep walking round, and the spirit of the show begins to seep into me. The more I see, the more a question formulates in my mind: do you really think they are riding for prizes and points? I think it is my problem and I am the one who needs to get a handle on these numbers.

It becomes clear to me that these are not soft, modern, aimless lives that Jocho and Mishima warn about. These riders are internally motivated with many different reasons for being out here.

These teachers are not prize chasers who foster competition and preach winning. They are not externally motivated either. They have inner guiding systems. Above all, I know they are not here for the marks and the prizes.

Being out among these people relieves me of my self-importance, and they teach me by their example. Inside I know that is how I also want to ride, eventually.

[102]

My long abstinences from competitive riding always had
their basis in the same particular American dilemma.
When I rode in competitions it seemed I should try to
win. In America winning is very important. Americans
have made folk heroes out of people like Vince Lom-
bardi, a famous professional football coach, whose
motto was 'Winning isn't everything, it is the only
thing'. On the other hand, I also knew what a bad
record the public and critics at large had in recognising
good work when it was right in front of them.

When, in my own competitions, I did try to win, and
even if I was successful, I had this instinctive suspicion
that someone was trying to force some doctrine on me.
Winning alone was too simplistic. It didn't take into
account any difference that two competitors might have
had at the start: how much harder one had to work than
the other, how far each had come, or if one just 'bought'
the win. The winner's crown was a light hat, often
decorated with the loud opinions and ideas of people
who usually never played the particular game they pro-
fessed to know so much about.

One day I saw an interview with a great Zen master,
Taisen Deshimaru. He was asked if he thought 'cham-
pionitis' could become a mental illness. He replied in
the affirmative, and went on to say that it was a narrow
vision of life. He said that the spirit of competition
today was often not good, and that the teachers were
partly responsible because they trained the body and
technique but did nothing for consciousness. As a result
their pupils fought to win like children playing war
games. He went on to say that there is no wisdom in
this approach and it is of no use at all in managing one's
own life.[4]

---

[4] DESHIMARU, TAISEN, *Zen and the Martial Arts*.

Deshimaru's words solidified many feelings for me. For one, it seemed someone older and wiser, a true master, had voiced a criticism of certain teachers which would have seemed impudent if it had come from a student. There was an element of relief in that alone. It vented some of my frustration and anger at those teachers who I felt deliberately mislead with their own biased certainty.

However, more important was that Deshimaru spoke of the same internal consciousness that Jocho and then Mishima did. I could see connections all around. I saw it as the same thing that every artist tries violently to protect – a free consciousness, a stream of consciousness, a subconsciousness. Here, at the junction, these became the pathway to the truth. They move farther and farther from contrivance and imitation, more and more towards true originality. A free consciousness is housed in a disciplined body like a queen bee in a hive. All the disciplined members nurture the queen, for she alone can create new life. The power to renew one's self, to create out of seemingly nothing, needs help. The true, total, person pays attention to technique and yet does not. There are many parts to the whole.

Finally I seemed to develop a sense of place for competitions. I thought they could be a place of action where good riding could be displayed. After all, if classical theory didn't work, it should be buried. However, I was convinced in the soundness of its elegant simplicity and its benefit to horses and riders. I began to see competitions as more of a display, an exhibition, more like a gallery, less like a contest. When I did resume riding in competitions, I knew I could never ride to win. I would ride instead not to lose. This was no trick of semantics. It was deadly serious. However, I was not talking about losing the competition. What I did not want to ever lose was my initial love of horses and riding, the excitement I had as a child. This turned out to be a far greater motivation, and an infinitely more difficult route.

Chapter Seven

Detraining the Mind – The Map is not the Territory

I AM AT A familiar place. I am digesting a lot of theory and literature in an effort to increase my knowledge and skill in riding. Since I have to work alone much of the time this is the only way I know. I often go to my practice with the movements I intend to ride idealised in my mind from the books I am reading. My plans seem good.

I begin riding. I try to train my horses to that pictured movement. I start comparing what is going on underneath me to the finished product in my head. The trouble is, nobody ever prints a photograph of a bad piaffe. All the books show exemplary movements, but none of the horses that I have begun in training re-create the perfect images that I have in my mind. Often my attempts are crude or out of balance. All I seem to see is how far off the mark my work is compared to my examples. After a while, this can get frustrating. I begin to wonder about the seemingly insurmountable gap between my day-to-day practice and these perfect descriptions and photographs.

Everything in my classic western education leads me to believe that, given enough analysis and thought, all apparent mysteries will yield. Nothing can ultimately escape from 'true scientific observation'. Look at western man's accomplishments: space travel, medicine, etc. All one has to do is exercise the mind. Eventually all the mysteries of the world will be explained. Or will they?

If you take up the study of riding through the information from its recorded literature, some certain mysterious holes appear in the fabric of its writings.

For hundreds of years the Spanish Riding School in Vienna has systematically prepared some of the best riders and horses. The web of knowledge that radiates from its disciples is immeasurable in its complexity and vastness. Its teachers have criss-crossed the globe, and these teachers in turn have prepared others who have become coaches, etc. The collective experience of the school, from generation to generation of horses and trainers, is immense. It seems inconceivable that a horse-training problem could exist which has not been corrected ten times over at this great School. It would seem logical that the School, like any other great learning institution, would have libraries full of treatises on every aspect of horsemanship. One would assume that it has produced volumes on the specific steps and correct principles of training the high school dressage horse. However, this is not the case at all. The sum total of the written directives of the Spanish Riding School amounts to literally a few pages. All the amazing consistency and knowledge is transmitted in some other way.

If you continue searching and reading, you cannot fail to notice the constant references to the universally accepted greatness of the French trainer, la Guerinière. However, if you try to find all the answers to specific riding problems in the wisdom of la Guerinière, you may be frustrated. La Guerinière did not leave us volumes and volumes. Furthermore, even though he was noted for the clarity of his work, it has still driven some more analytical modern horsemen to neurosis trying to prove or disprove what he said.

I have in front of me ten different dressage books, each with line drawings and photographs included, and the average number of pages in the books is 140. Ten different masters – and only these few pages. Even today one hears criticisms being made about some great living masters to the effect that they are not really that good because they are unable to express exactly what they do on the back of a horse.

I think this points to a paradox that the western mind does not like to entertain: namely, that observations about riding and riding are two very distinct and separate worlds.

Although we need to use words to learn and to teach, they still are very limited. Breaking up the dynamic movements of riding a horse into 'successive entities' in order to talk about it is very artificial. The flow of riding is too continuous to keep stopping it, chopping it up with analysis of particular movements separated from the whole.

It is no wonder I was so often frustrated with my riding and the horses' performances. My self-imposed projections about what the movements I went to practise should look like were unrealistic. Consequently there was always friction between reality and the mental image. There was no room to grow or to develop. If, for example, I go to practise the piaffe on a young horse and I have this specific idea of the piaffe I would like, a perfect image from some book, this is going to be trouble. For one thing no horse can perform such a finished product at the first attempts and furthermore even the trained horse cannot be expected to perform the same way every time out. As long as I keep this static image, usually a finished example, and try to imitate it, I will be unaware of what is going on in the present. I will be unaware of a particular horse's idiosyncrasies and likes and dislikes. Worse, I will be forgetting that the real essence is the process. The idea behind the piaffe is not to exhibit some kind of specifically calculated movement, for the sake of exhibition or the rider's ego. It is instead to perform a supreme exercise. The piaffe's real value lies in doing it, not in proving anything by exhibiting a trick. The piaffe's value is in the cumulative gymnastic effects it has on the horse. It has little value as something to be observed like a dead piece of art. Riding is a living art. For me this was a thorny issue. If you read books on riding you will often see, for example, separate chapters devoted to piaffe and passage, even entire books analysing specific placement of the legs and angulation. The unintended message, at least to me as an apprentice, is that somehow these movements are different and separate from all the other work. Unfortunately writings are notorious for breaking things up into 'successive entities', with few warnings as to how artificial these statements are.

It is my feeling that the limited amount of writings by the greatest riders and the greatest schools of riding is no accident. I believe the best teachers are much more interested in setting up situations where the student can learn for him/herself since it will be different for each and every one of us.

I think if one does not understand Korzybski's law 'the map is not the territory', or that talking about riding is not riding, one can get into some serious and expanding problems. Instead of your mind helping you ride, it will begin seriously to hinder you. You can suffer from paralysis by analysis. If, on the other hand, a teacher comes along and tells the rider to think of beautiful images, he is no better than the over-analytical non-rider. There is an important use for the mind in riding, but it is not to hold on to immobile projections, fixed images, etc., no matter whether they are under the guise of science, art, or philosophy. If there is an important use for the mind, then what is it?

In order to get some appreciation of the part to be played by the mind, let us take a quick look at the timing involved in certain movements. When performing single-time changes horse and rider can be executing two changes every second. Obviously the rider must have perfect timing and the horse must be responding instantaneously in order to execute new flying changes approximately every six tenths of a second. This gives one an impression of the speeds in the rider's reactions, as well as of the control needed, even at these kinds of speeds. Furthermore, incredible as it may seem, flying changes are not the most difficult movements to be performed. Others will call upon the rider to be reading and reacting so instantaneously that reacting is too slow a word. To execute under these conditions the rider must develop fierce concentration and if he is riding more than one horse per day, he must be able to maintain it for several hours.

What kind of concentration are we talking about? What is the essence of the right kind of concentration? Does this mean when you are riding you should try mentally to lock in on the exercise? If we zero in on an idea, will peripheral distractions lose their impact because we have something called up so solidly front and centre? Aren't the best concentrators the ones who can fix their attention unflinchingly on one particular task or idea or function?

In all the above instances, perceptions will be limited not enhanced, and reactions will be slowed down and not accelerated. Any time there is a strong focussing on one object or one idea, the result is an exclusion of other things in the vicinity. It doesn't matter what the idea is, even if it is the idea not to think about an idea. The more self-conscious, the more limitations. This kind of concentration can deaden the brain. Hypnosis requires this kind of initial focussing to work. Yogi's repetitive recantations of mantras can deaden the mind and body to external stimuli. This kind of concentration is not of much use when one is involved in unfolding, changing action. In fact in any dynamic situation like living or riding, it can be very harmful. In the world of action, one must become aware of everything simultaneously. In the best concentration you stop putting things into your mind. You try to cease the directives and analysis; you let the mind be free to do what it does best – and that is to perceive the entire world around you with all your senses at once. Because we are multisensory we can be receiving information etc. on several levels all at the same time. The result of the right concentration can be miraculous. In an open, alert but calm way the body can attain intuitive reactions which are not really reactions because there is no time lag between action and reaction. The horse and rider literally become one, feeling things at the same time. How could I develop this kind of concentration? This is what I was after.

There was a time on this earth when the correct kind of concentration was at a zenith. Several things conspired at once in feudal Japan to effect these incredible advances in concentration. Advances in concentration which demonstrated themselves in the advances of *joba-jutsu*, the major martial art of horsemanship, and in swordfighting, archery, etc. At this time thousands of Samurai fighters were employed by the feudal barons of Japan to protect and embellish their holding of lands and goods. Amazingly enough all Samurai used primarily the same kind of weapons in their battles: two swords. Since fighting was constant, there was obviously intense competition among these swordfighters, horsemen, archers. Weaknesses in technique were quickly and permanently culled in the endless battles. Anyone can imagine the seriousness with which Samurai practised their skills. Schools of technique flourished. In these life-and-death tests the teachings and teachers were also quickly weeded out. The level of skill in horsemanship, swordfighting and archery became very high. Anything that might give a Samurai an edge was intensely studied.

At the same time Zen Buddhism was continuing its development. Zen's firey insistency in being grounded in the real world, on being pragmatic and totally and immediately connected to the world, without cluttering mental philosophies, on being intuitive and natural, free if you will, finally came to the attention of some of the fighters. When these men undertook the study of Zen, a side-effect was an incredible improvement in their particular skill. Without cumbersome analysis of technique and forced manipulation their swordwork, like their lives, became elegantly simple; it became direct as a bolt of lightning. These swordsmen, horsemen and archers became legendary. Some became great teachers. Today *kendo* – swordfighting with bamboo swords – and the other martial arts are the direct descendants of this knowledge concerning the highest development of concentration.

It seemed clear to me that if I were having a problem with concentration and with getting a direct hold on knowledge, I had to pursue these Eastern teachings further. My mind was unsettled. My riding seemed to be pulled in many strange directions at once. It was in this mix, though, that I eventually came to my last lessons as an apprentice.

Chapter Eight

Breathing – A Half-halt for the Rider

AFTER I HAD BEGUN to pursue some of the Eastern teachings, one of my most important riding lessons came in an unusual form. It did not provide a particular answer to a specific problem, but more a way to look for answers. I realised that I would never progress if tension was inhibiting my actions and reactions. In an effort to reduce tension whenever it started to creep in I began using some traditional Japanese breathing exercises. When I started to use deliberate patterns of breathing, it had an almost instantaneous result. Within minutes, sometimes after only a few breaths, I could get myself to relax. Tension would usually build up in a similar fashion: the horse might be disobedient, or an exercise would fall apart – something would cause me to become frustrated. Without knowing it I would start to harden my posture. This muscular tightness would restrict my natural breathing. My form would deteriorate. Obviously as I became less flexible, my dexterity decreased. No matter who started this process, the end results were always the same stiffening effects. In its own right this kind of cycling aggravation is a problem; but when you couple it with the fact that some of the most difficult dressage movements not only require quick fluid executions of complicated combinations of legs, hands, and weight aids, but also a simultaneous wide open monitoring system, it then becomes obvious how even small amounts of tension will hinder the progress of the rider and confuse the horse.

The dressage rider must become more flexible, lighter, quicker and more pliant as the degree of difficulty increases – not harder, stiffer, and heavier.

With the introduction of breathing exercises, I could interrupt this negative chain of events early in the process. If I felt any restriction I began a series of breaths: deep, steady inhalation through the nose, a moment of holding, and then calm, deep exhalation through the mouth. This exhalation should not be forcefully restricted. (It is possible to increase the pressure in the chest

[115]

to the point where it can restrict blood flow back to the heart, and can cause dizziness.)

Koichi Tohei[1] recommends that this is practised sitting, until you can extend the cycle to approximately one breath per minute. He also notes this is only possible with practice and by keeping calm and by 'keeping one point'. Keeping one point can be roughly translated as keeping yourself centered in your abdomen. This happens to be the body's centre of gravity. In martial arts this centre controls and facilitates physical and psychic balance and is the place where all movement originates; it is the real master control centre. To me it is not a coincidence that in the proper dressage seat you are attempting to find this all the time. That is why I think breathing can be so effective to a rider.

Deep, efficient breathing helped my riding physically and psychologically. Physically, as the diaphragm muscle below the lungs contracts and flattens out, pulling fresh air into the lungs, it has the effect of compressing the organs below it. This can have the feeling of sinking the centre of gravity and internally deepening the rider's seat. I remember one time when Nuno Oliviera was making a point to students about the rider's seat. He was talking about each successive vertebra in one's back sinking into the next, and right down into the horse. I am certain that it was this idea of sinking one's centre of gravity, or at least focussing on it, that he was talking about. As the diaphragm contracts the upper rib cage is also expanding to further fill the lungs with the fresh air of every inhalation. In this part of the breath, I could hear Dr Van Schaik's favourite phrase, 'Make yourself tall', being repeated. He often talked about the very natural upward growth from the abdo-

[1] TOHEI, KOICHI, *Book of Ki: Coordinating Mind and Body in Daily Life*, Japan Publishing, Inc. 1976.

[116]

men to the chest which would seat the rider correctly over his seat bones. These pieces of advice were perfectly compatible with the anatomy of breathing. The result of the simple, but life-sustaining process was that in every single cycle of breathing, my posture had the chance of being naturally corrected – pelvis straightened, torso lengthened, shoulders opened. When I practised deeper, steady breathing it actually accentuated my position in the correct form.

Trained breathing helps develop the capacity of the heart and lungs thus increasing muscle fitness and developing a greater anaerobic threshold, so that the rider as an athlete is in better condition. Sheer physical strain is reduced by an increase in fitness. Psychologically, deep, efficient breathing grounded me. The mere fact of paying attention to breathing would adjust my awareness. When a problem loomed up and tried to command all of my mind's attention, it was my regular breathing that would reopen my total perception and unlock any stranglehold one particular dilemma might have had. Only if I were aware would I be able to ride my way to a solution.

To me as a rider, the effects of breathing seemed very analogous to the effect of the half-halt on the horse. Proper breathing alone has the power to rebalance the rider if he is leaning too far forward or back. Through its subtle constant corrections it can make the rider plumb. When breathing re-establishes the rider's psychological rhythm it acts exactly as the half-halt does in calming down a rushing or hurried horse. As the gait takes on its natural swinging pace, the rider's actions relax and smooth out. But breathing's most profound similarity to the half-halt is the way it can prepare the rider for a transition or any change. The attentive and aware rider is not surprised by something new. Sitting there in good balance the rider is expecting it.

Chapter Nine

Retraining the Mind – A Revelation of Centres

I HAD EXPRESSLY begun the study of martial arts to increase my concentration. I was sure I needed stronger powers of attention. I thought I needed more focussing so that I could hold my attention tighter for longer periods of time. I saw this flaw in my concentration as the latest hurdle of my apprenticeship. I was certain that this failing was inhibiting my riding and training. The interesting thing was that although I may have pinpointed the source of trouble, the correction was different to what I expected.

If I were doing a shoulder-in on a fairly green horse, and the horse slipped in and out of balance from three tracks to four then back to straightness, I always felt this was wrong. But how could it be wrong if it was all that the horse could give me at the time? As the horse became stronger and more flexible the movement would change. This business of isolating and then criticising a single movement in one moment of time was a very narrow vision, and pointed out a misunderstanding of the training process. The more I focussed on a concrete image in my mind of what was supposed to happen during my practice, the more disappointed I was when there was deviation from this ideal. Instead of keeping up with my awareness, this is where my concentration faltered. When, for example, I had trouble in movement one, I was carrying the mood into movement two and movement three and so on. In the past I always thought that my aggravation was due to a performance that was off the mark, unlike the photograph in my mind. This was only one part of it. The second part was practically a physical reaction. Getting stuck, agonising over a movement that didn't fit my idea, or someone else's, left me behind the immediate riding I was supposed to be doing. I lost my place in terms of feeling. All my senses became muddled fielding information, perceiving, but my mind stopped processing it as it was. Soon we were all out of synch. I was psychologically dizzy.

I was beginning to see that when you stop your mind to focus intently on something, it doesn't matter if it is in anger over a particular short-coming or if you are blindly pursuing a peaceful image: the result is the same.

You will be left behind the unfolding action of the here and now. This will make you late, and you will be aware of it. The horse seems to be riding off without you. Whenever I found myself way behind the action, I became confused, and rightly so. A flash of temper seemed to be an acknowledgment of this frustration and loss of control. Even the novice rider will be able to sense this discord and will want the harmony back – that feeling of fitting in with the horse and the world.

There was never anything drastically wrong with my concentration. Certainly there was not a need to be more focussed. In the world of action there just isn't time to be constantly reflecting, theorising, and wondering whilst riding. The more that I segmented the riding, isolating one movement from another, the more unconnected it all became. I had to approach it as a whole.

Throughout my apprenticeship I always was looking for concrete answers to my riding questions. Yet the farther I went, the more I began to get the feeling that the answers are more like questions and, at best, only suggestions. This illusiveness was very confusing to me as an apprentice. I could see that a lot of my impatience and intolerance was with the imprecision of learning and the training process; the illusiveness of things always changing, always in motion. By the time I had arrived at Maruyama's dojo, I began to get the feeling that the right concentration comes from a confidence that you will let yourself do the right thing. The art of riding is an art in motion. I had to become secure to live with the illusiveness of all of this movement. I had to stop limiting my work by seeing it in a preconceived way. Nothing was going to fit the images of my mind's eye. Nor would it fit a picture of another rider on another horse in another moment of time. I had to let myself try. Deep down inside, from very early in my apprenticeship, I knew how serious these steps were that I had been taking. There is no turning back when you start to walk into your own circle, and away from the circle of your teachers. You take responsibility for what might happen next. The swift river moves before you; its bottom is full of slippery rocks. You walk along the banks looking for a bridge across, but there is none. If you want to experience the other side, you have to wade in. You know very well that with one slip you will go under, but you decide to try.

It was in Maruyama's dojo that my apprenticeship ended. In Maruyama's dojo, there she was. As I watched this woman's swordwork, and her teaching, I saw grace and beauty, fearlessness, and femininity. So many things about her seemed balanced. I found myself admiring her. As I talked with her, something serious locked into place. I saw that she must have faced tremendous pressure to surrender to a system which seemed to demand that women never assert. As she became more and more adept she must have appeared threatening to many people who had fixed ideas about frail femininity. Who could say how much she had doubted her own femininity as she progressed towards becoming a martial artist? I wondered where she gathered strength to pursue her path when it was dark and she felt alone.

Now anyone could see what a beautiful woman she had become. Her strength did not detract from her femininity. It enhanced it. Her power gave her femininity more drama and depth. She could stand like a lioness. From her long study of fighting she had learned to command respect and exude a comforting peacefulness.

I saw then the mirror struggle within myself against a system suggesting and supporting power, force, domination and aggression in a man. My job, even when I didn't know it, often involved learning not to be afraid of softness; being comfortable in allowing softness and intuition a place to thrive in the sphere that was me. I had not only to let it exist, but also, like the great Japanese wrestlers who study gentle painting, I, too, had to cultivate the opposites in order to develop my balance.

My admiration for this woman helped me. As I admired her work and saw the similarities of our struggles, I could admire my own work. I seemed to be able to accept my own work just as it was. In that small understanding I set myself free from my constant goals and expectations. I saw clearly that just as she was the centre of her own struggle, I was the centre of mine. And every other learner had his or her centre. Each was the centre of her/his own universe. There was not just one centre of the universe. There were millions, side by side, coexisting simultaneously. I saw the universality of all apprenticeship struggles, the similarity of all of our roads. We are all alone, and yet there are many of us out there. We could inspire each other with the spirit and integrity of our work, or we could presume, criticise and judge. If a horseman has an abiding respect for his or her own road, then it must show in the respect for others and for the horse. We can never really compete against each other because we are all on different roads. To be a real horseman I knew I would have to keep a careful check on my own ideas and ego and have true respect for the horse's life.

The study of technique and the practice of form gives the body awareness. It cannot be stopped. Whether you are ready or not you will be able to feel things outside your own body. The first cracks in the bubble of yourself will appear. Your awareness grows until you are capable of transcending yourself on horseback. You can move out of your own self centre, out of your ego. It

[123]

will be up to you to take that step and go along. The beauty of the paradox is that as soon as you disconnect from yourself you don't despair but you immediately connect with everything around you. In the right concentration your whole being is listening. You really connect with your horse. Once you can move out of yourself, there is nothing stopping how much you can learn. Without presumption anything is possible. Nothing is strange. Answers, at best, are temporary and questions become more comfortable.

In Maruyama's dojo not only was I making peace with myself but also I was making peace with the learning process. I wouldn't need the constant attention of a teacher any more. I would be able to work alone. Whether you think you know the solution to a problem, or whether you don't, you still must ride the same way. The object is not to get someone to give you the answer, the idea is to figure out your own answers. You cannot think up an answer to every riding problem. You must ride through a riding problem. That is the training process, and the word dressage means training. It is dressage itself which answers its own questions.

As I left I felt very drained, and tired. Something seemed missing. I felt emotionally exhausted. I even felt empty. I also noticed I was very calm. I didn't have any particular answers in mind, but I didn't have any questions either.

I knew that tomorrow I would be riding again. I walked through several blocks of the harsh city. The sun was setting. I got into my car and began the drive home. The sun came in strongly through my windscreen as I travelled west. I thought back to when I was twelve years old. I remembered the first time that the man I worked for in the summers let me go riding by myself. It was in the rolling hills of the New York Finger Lakes country. I rode down an abandoned dirt road out to a section of woods above the long lake. Some of these paths could have been traversed by the members of the great Seneca Indian nation, part of the Iroquois sisterhood that stretched across all of what is now New York State. Small brown puffs of dust rose up behind the footfalls of the horse. Hawks were circling low in the evening sky. How much wiser I seemed then. So excited. So satisfied just to be on the back of a horse, riding towards the light.

Epilogue

I WOULD LIKE TO be able to say that immediately after my experience in Mr Maruyama's training hall, completing what I have called my apprenticeship, I was overcome with joy and celebration.

I guess I always expected it to end like some graduation ceremony – throwing hats into the air in jubilation. Maybe I should have received a piece of paper stating the privileges attached to this culmination. But who would have issued it?

It wasn't like that. And learning the art is not like that. It can never be measured by examinations. The true feeling was more like a sense of peace. I don't mean to suggest some overly romantic, calm, god-like trance. I am talking more about a kind of important relief. Imagine that for years and years there had been a constant background noise in your ears. You had grown accustomed to it and could function in spite of it. Yet you were always aware it was there. Then one day you found it had gone. Your reaction would not be jubilation. It would be more one of disbelief, scepticism; you might sit for a minute and just relish the relief. You might expect the sound to come back at any moment. With each new day you would begin to see how much of a hold it had on you. Your confidence would grow as you began to really live without it.

What I saw was that knowledge, or wisdom, seemed to be following exactly the lessons of riding. The idea of breaking down the process of learning into grades and degrees, those 'successive entities' again, was just as artificial as breaking down the piaffe or passage.

I was beginning to see wisdom, knowledge, as a fundamental way of being or looking; a process not an end result. The best teachers were always above all the best learners. In fact as far as I could see they were learners first and always, no matter how old they were or how much they already knew.

So when I say there was no great joy, elation or celebration of the completion of a course of training or learning, it was as much because I finally perceived that everything was really just beginning. Certainly I wasn't unhappy.

Why did I think this realisation, this graduation, should be more dramatic? What could be more dramatic than to realise that I would never know an ending in riding, that I would always be beginning? What in the end could be more profound than to go to my regular work each day with the excitement and innocence of a beginner?